Inter te**X**t

The Language of Advertising

This accessible satellite textbook in the Routledge INTERTEXT series is unique in offering students hands-on practical experience of textual analysis focused on written advertisements. Written in a clear, user-friendly style by an experienced writer and teacher, it combines practical activities with texts, followed by commentaries to show how messages are constructed from language and suggestions for research. It can be used individually or in conjunction with the series core textbook, *Working with Texts*.

Aimed at A-Level and beginning undergraduate students, *The Language of Advertising*:

◎   focuses on the interrelation of language, image and layout
◎   explores the discourse between 'reader' and advertisement
◎   examines advertising strategies such as hooklines, puns and connotations
◎   looks at the relationship between advertising and culture
◎   draws on literary and linguistic theory for analysis of texts
◎   includes a wide range of advertisements from British Airways to Castlemaine XXXX
◎   has a comprehensive glossary of terms

Angela Goddard is Senior Lecturer in Language at the Centre for Human Communication, Manchester Metropolitan University, and was a Chief Moderator for the project element of the English Language A Level for twelve years.

'Angela Goddard is an outstanding educator; the book captures her strengths: clarity, rigour, practical relevance and FUN.'
        David Hurry, *Sheffield Hallam University*

The Intertext series

◎ **Why does the phrase 'spinning a yarn' refer both to using language and making cloth?**

◎ **What might a piece of literary writing have in common with an advert or a note from the milkman?**

◎ **What aspects of language are important to understand when analysing texts?**

The Routledge INTERTEXT series will develop readers' understanding of how texts work. It does this by showing some of the designs and patterns in the language from which they are made, by placing texts within the contexts in which they occur, and by exploring relationships between them.

The series consists of a foundation text, *Working with Texts: A core book for language analysis*, which looks at language aspects essential for the analysis of texts, and a range of satellite texts. These apply aspects of language to a particular topic area in more detail. They complement the core text and can also be used alone, providing the user has the foundation skills furnished by the core text.

Benefits of using this series:

◎ **Unique** – written by a team of respected teachers and practitioners whose ideas and activities have also been trialled independently

◎ **Multi-disciplinary** – provides a foundation for the analysis of texts, supporting students who want to achieve a detailed focus on language

◎ **Accessible** – no previous knowledge of language analysis is assumed, just an interest in language use

◎ **Comprehensive** – wide coverage of different genres: literary texts, notes, memos, signs, advertisements, leaflets, speeches, conversation

◎ **Student-friendly** – contains suggestions for further reading; activities relating to texts studied; commentaries after activities; key terms highlighted and an index of terms

The series editors:

Ronald Carter is Professor of Modern English Language in the Department of English Studies at the University of Nottingham and is the editor of the Routledge INTERFACE series in Language and Literary Studies. He is also co-author of *The Routledge History of Literature in English*. From 1989 to 1992 he was seconded as National Director for the Language in the National Curriculum (LINC) project, directing a £21.4 million in-service teacher education programme.

Angela Goddard is Senior Lecturer in Language at the Centre for Human Communication, Manchester Metropolitan University, and was Chief Moderator for the project element of English Language A-Level for the Northern Examination and Assessment Board (NEAB) from 1983 to 1995. Her publications include *The Language Awareness Project: Language and Gender*, vols I and II, 1988, and *Researching Language*, 1993 (Framework Press).

First series title:

Working with Texts: A core book for language analysis
Ronald Carter, Angela Goddard, Danuta Reah, Keith Sanger, Maggie Bowring

Satellite titles:

The Language of Sport
Adrian Beard

The Language of Advertising: Written texts
Angela Goddard

The Language of Poetry
John McRae

The Language of Newspapers
Danuta Reah

The Language of Humour
Alison Ross

The Language of Fiction
Keith Sanger

Related titles:

INTERFACE series:

Variety in Written English
Tony Bex

Language, Literature and Critical Practice
David Birch

A Linguistic History of English Poetry
Richard Bradford

The Language of Jokes
Delia Chiaro

The Discourse of Advertising
Guy Cook

Literary Studies in Action
Alan Durant and Nigel Fabb

English in Speech and Writing
Rebecca Hughes

Feminist Stylistics
Sara Mills

Language in Popular Fiction
Walter Nash

Textual Intervention
Rob Pope

The Language of Advertising

Written texts

- Angela Goddard

LONDON AND NEW YORK

First published 1998
by Routledge
11 New Fetter Lane, London EC4P 4EE

Simultaneously published in the USA and Canada
by Routledge
29 West 35th Street, New York, NY 10001

Reprinted 1998

© 1998 Angela Goddard

Typeset in Stone Sans/Stone Serif by Solidus (Bristol) Limited
Printed and bound in Great Britain by Redwood Books, Trowbridge, Wiltshire

British Library Cataloguing in Publication Data
A catalogue record for this book is available from the British Library

Library of Congress Cataloging in Publication Data
A catalog record for this book is available from the Library of Congress

ISBN 0–415–14598–8

contents

acknowledgements

Maria Forser and Dr Shelagh Warme: for analysis and translation of the Swedish advert, p. 98.
Ron Goddard: for the e-mail letter, p. 50.
A big thank you to everyone who contributed ideas to this book, and who read and commented on drafts, particularly the following people: Adrian Beard, Ronald Carter, Danuta Reah and Keith Sanger.

The following illustrations and texts have been reprinted by courtesy of their copyright holders:
Saatchi advert: Saatchi & Saatchi
Tobacco: Tobacco Manufacturer's Association
Newspaper article: The *Independent*
NSPCC (1): NSPCC
InterCity: British Railways Board
Harveys Bristol Cream: Allied Domecq
Charity appeal: Leukaemia Research
British Airways (1): British Airways
British Airways (2): British Airways
Fictive dialogue (extract from Pat Barker's *Union Street*): Virago Press
Delia Smith recipes (extract from Delia Smith's *Winter Collection*): Delia Smith, copyright 1995, with the permission of BBC Worldwide Limited
Banking Direct: Bank of Scotland
BP: BP Oil
ICI: ICI
Castlemaine XXXX: Carlsberg-Tetley
Time magazine: Saatchi & Saatchi
NSPCC (2): NSPCC
Photo of Susannah Hart, Interbrand Director: photographer Richard Kalina
Lavvo: *Woman and Home* 1937
Tampax: Abbott, Mead Vickers. BBDO Ltd
Older adverts: *Woman and Home* 1937–50
IL Returpapper: Returpapper
Allinson's: Allied Bakeries Ltd
Lea & Perrins: HP Foods Ltd

The publishers have made every effort to contact copyright holders, although this has not been possible in all cases. Outstanding permissions will be remedied in future editions. Please contact the Textbook Development Editor at Routledge.

introduction

This book has already advertised itself to you. Here are some of its strategies:

Make no mistake : advertising works. However, as a culture, we tend to be aloof and not a little snooty about advertisements, pretending that, while they may work on *some* people, they don't work on *us*, and dismissing advertising language as trite discourse written for the uneducated.

Beyond the single example of this book's marketing strategies, there is much evidence that advertising works on a whole variety of people, and in surprisingly immediate ways. For instance, when British Telecom TV advertisements propose to us the benefits of making phone calls, we make more phone calls; when the Post Office reminds us of the enjoyment that getting a letter brings, we put pen to paper; in 1985, when a TV commercial featured a young man stripping down to his underwear in a launderette in order to wash his Levi 501s, sales of that brand of jeans went from 80,000 to 650,000 pairs over the course of one year (Sebag-Montefiore 1987).

Product manufacturers would not invest in advertisements if they didn't work, and the sums of money invested can be enormous: for example, in 1990, British Airways launched its 'Global' TV commercial, which was filmed by Hugh Hudson (the director of *Chariots of Fire*) in the Utah desert with a cast of 4,000 extras dressed in red, white and blue, coming together with firm handshakes and friendly embraces. The sequence, set to operatic music, and finishing with an aerial shot of a winking face made up of the people involved (see Text: Saatchi advert), was planned to a budget of £14 million for production and the first year of transmission. Saatchi and Saatchi, the agency who created the advert, aimed to reach 600 million viewers during that year.

The difference between such an epic production and the local homespun written advertisement may appear to be huge, but both types of text require us, as readers, to interact with them, and this can often be a very complex process – far removed from the idea of adverts as simple texts for the simple-minded. In terms of visual codes, the reader works to create meaning from given items – for example, the visual signs of the winking face and the handshake suggest certain ideas. But meanings are not fixed for all readers : a wink and a handshake will have no meaning to a cultural group who do not have these signs in their communication system. Even within a single culture, there are likely to be different readings: for example, the hands clasped in handshake are male, and as such are likely to produce a different reading by a female reader from that produced by a male.

While any reading of image needs to consider the different perspectives that readers bring, the same level of complexity often surrounds the verbal language in a text. Advertising copywriters regularly produce texts which are as highly wrought as any piece of

Text: Saatchi advert

literature, using fully the resources of language and inviting creative and subtle readings from their users.

Although advertisements are ephemeral in that each one is short-lived, their effects are longstanding and cumulative: they leave traces of themselves behind, which combine to form a body of messages about the culture that produced them. These messages can then function both to reflect and to construct cultural values: they can reflect the values of the powerful groups in society who produced the texts, but the reflection itself can then harden to become the touchstone for everyone.

The position of this book is that advertisements are forms of discourse which make a powerful contribution to how we construct our

Text: Saatchi advert

identities. At the same time, for adverts to work, they must use our commonly shared resources of language in ways that affect us and mean something to us. These two aspects of analysis should be inextricable – part of the task of looking at the message should involve paying attention to how it is delivered. While many books have looked at advertising, fewer have paid any detailed attention to how messages are constructed from language. This is what makes this particular book different from others.

In advertising terms, this element of difference would be called the book's **Unique Selling Proposition.** If you have been persuaded, then read on ...

What is an advertisement?

Advertising is so familiar to modern readers that it may seem odd to ask what an advertisement is. Although advertising is all around us – perhaps *because* it is all around us – we don't often pause to think about its nature as a form of discourse, as a system of language use whereby, on a daily basis, huge numbers of readers have fleeting 'conversations' with the writers of countless texts.

This unit aims to examine the extent of this daily discourse, and to draw some conclusions about how we might define the act of communication we call 'advertising'.

We all recognise the type of advertising text that occurs in newspapers and magazines, where a product is being presented as desirable for us to buy; we also know the TV version of this, placed between the programmes on certain channels. But should our classification be wider than that?

5

Below are some examples of texts that we might see around us on a daily basis. The word 'text' here is used in its widest sense, including visual artifacts as well as verbal language. Which of these would you call 'advertisements', and which not? Justify your inclusion (and exclusion) of texts by explaining the criteria you are using in your classification. Add any further texts not mentioned here that you think ought to be part of your list.

◎   A university prospectus
◎   A political manifesto
◎   A film trailer
◎   A 'speed limit' road sign
◎   A manufacturer's label sewn on the outside of clothes – e.g. on jeans or trainers
◎   A shop name on a carrier bag
◎   A poster in the grounds of a church, with 'Jesus Lives' written on it
◎   A T-shirt with a slogan on it – e.g. 'Time to Party'

Commentary

Classifying texts in this way is more complex than it may seem at first glance, because as soon as we try to arrive at a satisfactory system we bring into play important ideas about the role texts perform in particular contexts – in other words, about how they appear and are used. Another complication is the fact that texts don't always fall neatly into categories according to purpose. Texts are hardly ever simply 'informative' or 'persuasive', for example. Information texts, such as university prospectuses, always have an individual or corporate perspective behind them; persuasive texts, such as political manifestos or film trailers, often do their job by the way they present information.

At the root of the word 'advertisement' is the Latin verb 'advertere', meaning 'to turn towards'. While it is undoubtedly true that adverts are texts that do their best to get our attention, to make us turn towards them, we wouldn't want to say that everything we pay attention to is an advert. For example, road signs such as the 'speed limit' one on the list above try to get our attention as an essential part of their function, but we don't perceive them as advertising anything. Often, though, our classifications are more a question of degree than of absolutes. For example, clothing in its broadest sense can be seen as advertising ideas about the wearer, but manufacturers' labels on our clothing are a very direct strategy for them to get themselves some free publicity, and this is no different from the names we are forced to carry around on our plastic bags.

Central to our idea of an advert appears to be the factor of conscious intention behind the text, with the aim of benefiting the originator materially or through some other less tangible gain, such as enhancement of status or image. So, although a church poster might not be selling us anything in the material sense, it is still intentionally selling an idea – religion – in order to benefit the institution of the church by drawing converts and swelling its ranks.

Of all the texts on this list, the T-shirt is arguably the most complicated. We might decide that it is a form of advertising, but, unless we talk to the wearer, we are unlikely to be sure who is advertising what: is the manufacturer advertising itself on an unwitting subject, or is the wearer using the T-shirt to advertise some quality he or she supposedly possesses, such as party-going inclinations?

Activity

During the course of one day, log all the written texts you encounter that you would consider to be forms of advertising. Where possible, collect some of these texts. Try to arrive at a classification for the texts according to:

1   what is being advertised – a product, an idea, an image?
2   who is being addressed?

One aspect which you will have had to give some detailed thought to in your collection of advertisements is the notion of audience – item 2 above. As with literary texts, advertisements often have complex sets of addressers and addressees. For example, rather than there being one single voice in a text sending a message to a single group of people, there might be several different voices, more than one message, and a number of different audience groups. The next activity will explore this idea through some practical analysis.

Activity

Read Text: Tobacco carefully, then think about who is talking to whom. This will involve thinking about all the different elements of address relationship, as above. If it helps, draw a diagram to illustrate the different elements you identify. For example:

Addresser(s)   **Message**   **Addressee(s)**

7

Text: Tobacco

Tobacconists. Spot the difference and save £400.

The difference between selling cigarettes to someone over 16 and selling them to someone under 16 can be a £400 fine.
ISSUED BY THE TOBACCO ADVISORY COUNCIL FOR THE BRITISH TOBACCO INDUSTRY

The first noticeable addresser/addressee relationship is that within the photo story. There are two conversations here, the first where the tobacconist agrees to the boy's request and the second where he doesn't. We can only make sense of these interactions – and therefore understand their overall message – if we link them to the next address relationship that occurs in the advertisement: the Tobacco Advisory Council talking to tobacconists. The wording between the visual texts addresses tobacconists directly and orders them to read the photo stories and 'spot the difference'. We understand the latter phrase to refer to a particular kind of competition, where readers win a prize if they can identify the differences between near-identical photographs or drawings. Here, however, the task seems over-simple: all tobacconist-competitors have to do is to spot that 'yes' has turned to 'no' in the tobacconist's speech-bubble.

There are other things wrong with this competition, too. For example, instead of winning something, competitors are said to save £400. As general readers within the third address relationship, that of the Tobacco Advisory Council talking to the general public, we draw certain conclusions about why the message to tobacconists appears to be breaking these rules: in making the 'spot the difference' task so easy, the Tobacco Advisory Council is saying that it doesn't require much effort and vigilance on the part of tobacconists to refuse to sell cigarettes to underage customers. This enables us (the general public) to observe the Tobacco Advisory Council as a responsible body which acts to remind tobacco outlets, in turn, of their responsibilities. (There is a possible fourth address relationship, too: the Tobacco Advisory Council reminding young people under the age of 16 that it is illegal for them to buy cigarettes.)

In using a photo story format and in making the 'spot the difference' task so easy, the advertisement conveys the Tobacco Advisory Council's message in a humorous way, presenting its voice as authoritative but not authoritarian. At the same time, it is made clear that for tobacconists not to 'spot the difference' in terms of customers' ages is a serious matter: 'The difference between selling cigarettes to someone over 16 and selling them to someone under 16 can be a £400 fine.'

This advertisement is a good example of a text that is not selling a product, but rather an idea or image: we learn, through the various levels of address, that the British tobacco industry takes its responsibilities seriously enough to spend money making sure that those who are at the retail end of the organisation do not break the law.

9

Summary

This unit has suggested that advertising is not just about the commercial promotion of branded products, but can also encompass the idea of texts whose intention is to enhance the image of an individual, group or organisation.

In the process, the idea of advertisements as simple texts which operate on a single level has been challenged: instead, advertising texts are seen as potentially involving complex notions of audience, where readers have to work hard to decode messages and understand different address relationships.

While these ideas will be further developed at various points throughout this book, the next unit looks specifically at a range of attention-seeking devices used in advertisements to make the reader want to start the decoding process in the first place.

Attention-seeking devices

In Unit 1, it was pointed out that the terms 'advertisement' and 'advertising' have, at their root, a Latin word, 'advertere', meaning 'turn towards'. This unit will focus on some of the strategies used by advertising copywriters in their attempts to capture our attention.

It is not difficult to see why advertisers should want to make their texts capture our attention. The whole aim of the copywriters is to get us to register their communication either for purposes of immediate action or to make us more favourably disposed in general terms to the advertised product or service. But increasingly, written advertisements have to compete with each other and with all sorts of other texts in our richly literate culture. So copywriters have to find ways to shout at us from the page.

IMAGE

One attention-seeking strategy developed in recent years to increasing levels of sophistication is the startling image. The Benetton clothing company, for example, showed a series of large-scale hoardings which featured real scenes of life and death – a baby being born, covered in blood from the mother's womb, a man on his deathbed. The outcry of public offence which followed these advertisements drew yet more attention to them. Since the Benetton adverts, a number of different companies (for example, 18–30 Holidays and Gossard) have appeared to use the strategy of deliberately upsetting, outraging or otherwise irritating the general public in order to draw some extra attention.

It is very revealing of a culture's prevailing ideologies to consider what is thought shockingly unacceptable and what gets accepted as just bold, if a bit risqué. At the time of writing, women have been used as sexual commodities for many years in the selling of products as disparate as cars and chocolate bars. But male bodies have hitherto been off limits. Things appear to be changing, however. In the search for fresh ways of startling, advertisers seem to have realised that the male physique is uncharted territory. Text: Newspaper article below possibly illustrates this territory starting to be colonised.

Adverts can sometimes want to shock the reader for very good reasons, however increasingly, charities and other fund-raising groups have used some of the traditional methods of commercial product advertising to get their campaign noticed, and one of these methods has been the disturbing image, as a way of presenting the case for the need for support.

Activity

Read Text: NSPCC (1), and consider the following questions:

◎ Is the effectiveness of the advert simply to do with the image presented?

◎ How does the reader come to understand the message in this advert: which parts of the text did you read in which order, and how did you relate these parts to each other?

◎ Is there a difference, in your opinion, between this type of image and the type used by companies like Benetton?

Hello boys...but it's goodbye girls

Marianne Macdonald
Media Correspondent

Sizing them up: Deep cleavage is OK, but a smaller model is ordered for the underpants

Is it more acceptable to show a woman in a brassière on an advertising hoarding than a man in underpants?

An underwear company is grappling with the apparent sexism at the heart of this question after being warned off running a poster campaign showing a male model wearing underpants.

Its proposed slogans of "The Loin King" and "Full Metal Packet" are thought too cheeky, so to speak. But are they more so than the Wonderbra advert which shot Eva Herzigova's cleavage to fame under the legend "Hello Boys"?

Kevin Higgs, founder of Brass Monkeys, said that the Committee of Advertising Practice (CAP), an advisory arm of the Advertising Standards Author-

ity (ASA), told him he should use a "smaller" model if he wanted his poster campaign to run, despite its appearance without problems in men's magazines.

He wants to know why the makers of the Wonderbra advertisement were not given the same advice. "It's double standards. If it was female underwear, it wouldn't be a problem," he said yesterday. "They are probably all old men at the ASA who think it's fine to have a sexy looking female for men to look at, but you couldn't trust ladies on the high street with a picture of a good-looking man. It's ridiculous."

Mr Higgs said that members of CAP told him that an advertisement for Club 18-30, which featured a man's crotch over the slogan "Girls. Can we interest you in a package

holiday?" had also had to be withdrawn.

"I said, we're doing men's underwear. What do they want us to do? We can hardly put the underpants on his head."

A spokesman for the committee explained breasts were considered more acceptable than groins. "People will appreciate there's a difference between focusing on the groin area and the chest area in advertising," he said. But Susie Orbach, the best-selling feminist writer, said the ASA's distinction was bizarre. "We take it so much for granted that we can display and sell women's bodies that we don't even pause for thought. It takes trying to sell men through thier bodies to make us pay attention."

13

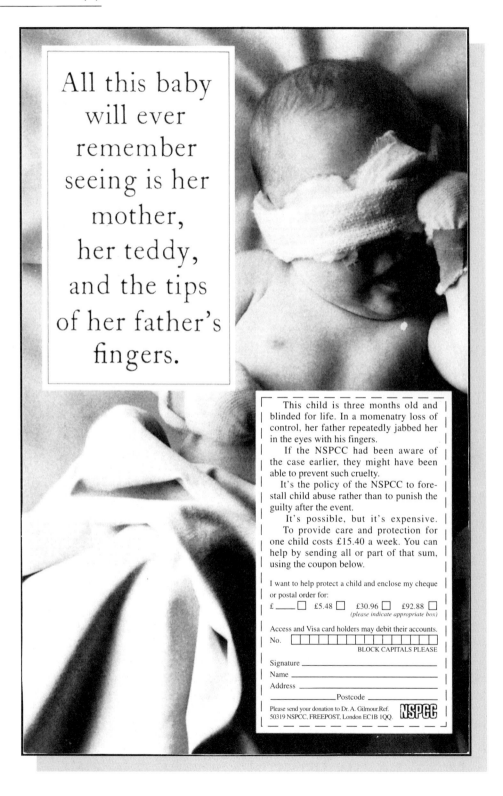

All this baby will ever remember seeing is her mother, her teddy, and the tips of her father's fingers.

This child is three months old and blinded for life. In a momenatry loss of control, her father repeatedly jabbed her in the eyes with his fingers.

If the NSPCC had been aware of the case earlier, they might have been able to prevent such cruelty.

It's the policy of the NSPCC to fore-stall child abuse rather than to punish the guilty after the event.

It's possible, but it's expensive.

To provide care and protection for one child costs £15.40 a week. You can help by sending all or part of that sum, using the coupon below.

I want to help protect a child and enclose my cheque or postal order for:

£ _____ ☐   £5.48 ☐   £30.96 ☐   £92.88 ☐
(please indicate appropriate box)

Access and Visa card holders may debit their accounts.

No. ☐☐☐☐☐☐☐☐☐☐☐☐☐☐☐☐
BLOCK CAPITALS PLEASE

Signature _____

Name _____

Address _____

_____ Postcode _____

Please send your donation to Dr. A. Gilmour.Ref. **NSPCC**
50319 NSPCC, FREEPOST, London EC1B 1QQ.

Commentary

Although this image is, at first glance, upsetting, the full extent of its meaning is not apparent until the reader has made sense of the verbal text. To this extent, the image is very different from one which stands alone and is simply designed to shock and get attention.

We register the fact that something has happened to this baby's eyes. There is a strong interactive dimension in the image as a result of the way the baby is trying to touch the bandages round her eyes with her hand, as if to comprehend what has happened to her. Her mouth is slightly open as if she wants to express something. She appears in a way that suggests we could communicate with her, if only we knew how and if only our message could be a hopeful one. The bandages look old fashioned and home made; the image would have created a very different effect if the scene had been a high-tech hospital room, full of monitoring apparatus, with the baby on her back and with her face turned away. As readers, we are interpreting here what is often called **paralanguage**. This is an umbrella term for those aspects of communication that surround and support our verbal language in normal face-to-face encounters: for example body position, gesture, physical proximity, clothing, touch, eye contact. This baby cannot communicate with us, but the fact that she is pictured as if she could (or wants to) is an important contribution to the overall effect of the image, because it makes us interactive partners in the communication process, and we realise gradually, as we read the verbal message, that her communicative potential has been forever impaired.

English speakers are used to reading text from left to right, working progressively down the page. The verbal text in the box, top left, is therefore in prime reading position. We realise that the baby is blind, and are told she will have a visual memory of only a limited number of things. These appear to be friendly, loving items – her mother, her teddy. But *the tips of her father's fingers* form a strange third element here. At this point, we perhaps think the baby has had an accident, and her father's fingers were the last thing she saw because he was trying to save her. At the same time, the phrase is oddly disturbing: why 'tips', why not 'her father's hands' or 'her father's fingers'? Why not just 'her father'?

When we get to the text bottom right, the puzzling nature of this phrase is explained. The text here is very sparse, paring down rather than embellishing in any sensational way what has happened. The effect is to suggest restraint and control of emotion, even a certain matter-of-factness on the part of the NSPCC: this is all-too-common an event, but one where they are not sitting in judgement. What has happened is 'cruelty', and the horror of it is certainly suggested by the phrase

15

'repeatedly jabbed'; but the baby's father had a 'momentary loss of control'. The text makes clear the horrific nature of his action while at the same time not demonising him. This makes it more possible for us to relate to the catastrophe: while we may not ourselves have done anything like this, we may well have experienced 'a momentary loss of control' from which something serious might have resulted. The visual text evokes our sense of protection, and the verbal text tells us how close to home that protection might need to be. Our donation is that protection from the worst aspect of our own human nature.

VERBAL TEXT

The focus so far has been on the idea of images as attention-seeking devices. In the previous activity, it should have become clear that readers do not simply read images in isolation from the verbal text that accompanies them; nor do they read the verbal text without reference to accompanying images.

Just as the way an image is presented can suggest certain ideas, such as the human vulnerability conveyed in the previous advert, so the verbal language can suggest particular qualities as a result of how it appears: in other words, writing is a form of image-making, too. It could be said to have its own paralanguage, as a result of the type of 'clothing' the copywriter has chosen for it.

One sharp distinction in how writing appears is whether it is handwriting or typed print, since we are likely to read handwriting as more to do with human agency and therefore more personal and individualistic than machine-produced typeface. These boundaries of 'human' and 'non-human' are, of course, constructed notions in contemporary society: we have mechanised ways of producing personalised-looking handwriting, and there is a human individual writing what you are reading now. This handwriting versus typed print distinction also masks lots of subtle variation. Different forms of handwriting are likely to suggest different types of author – for example, a rounded, joined-up script with 'footballs' or 'hearts' for dots over the letter 'i' may connote a young writer while an italicised print may suggest someone older; in terms of typeface, too, we are likely to have subtly different readings of different fonts (Helvetica)

different fonts (Times)

different fonts (Courier)

different styles (Italic)

different styles (Outline)

different styles (Shadow)

different sizes (12 point)

different sizes (18 point)

different sizes (24 point)

and also whether the typeface is emboldened (Bold),

quite aside from all the aspects of meaning we can suggest with UPPER-CASE and lower-case letters,

and ... features of punctuation?
and – features of punctuation!
and: 'features' of punctuation;
and features of 'punctuation'.

Activity

Look at Text: Intercity.
　　Now look back at the NSPCC advert.
　　Now look once again at the Intercity advert.
　　Think about the emotional effect each has had on you.
　　You could say that the two adverts have the theme of childhood in common – but there the similarity stops. Text: Intercity takes the idea of play, fun and fantasy whereas the previous text was concerned with vulnerability; whereas the previous text looked at the way in which adults can abuse children, this text looks at the way in which adults can *be* children.
　　To think further about the role of **typographical** features and their

17

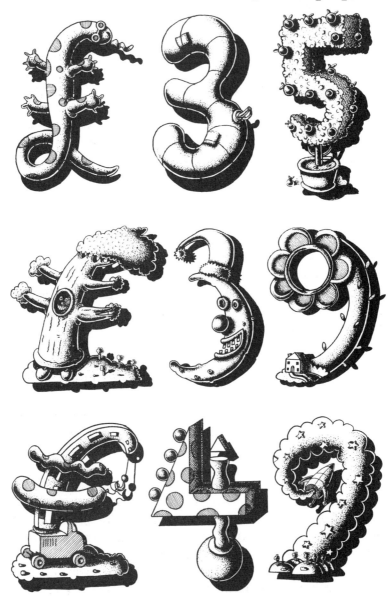

London return at very silly prices.

Just book your APEX ticket seven days in advance and you can travel from Glasgow to London return for £35, from Edinburgh for £39 or from Inverness for **£49.** From Glasgow or Edinburgh, APEX returns to Manchester are just £15 away or Birmingham £25. (Subject to availability). And, all these fares include **free** seat reservations. Have we gone completely loco? Pick up a leaflet for details from your station or Travel Agent.

INTERCITY

18

effects, look back at the NSPCC advert and examine the typeface used, particularly in the box top left in the text. How would you describe it? (You don't need to have a name for it – an impressionistic description will do). Now think how inappropriate it would be here to have the typeface used in the Intercity text: the fact that we would feel this to be offensive, given the message of the NSPCC advert, shows what strong connotations we ascribe to the different visual effects of typographical presentation.

Now look again at the Intercity advert. This time read each figure more carefully. What aspects of children's stories and toys are being used, in order to create the idea of 'silly prices'?

(Note: there is no commentary on this activity.)

LAYOUT

In addition to the effects that can be created by the choice of particular typographical features, writing can also be used to create larger textual shapes by means of different layouts. In this respect, adverts sometimes come very close to the way concrete poetry works - as verbal language making pictures of its own subject matter.

Activity

Look at Text: Harvey's Bristol Cream. The bottle shape is created in the vertical sense by the substitution of alternative place names for the 'Bristol' of the brand name. Note also, though, the 3-D effect created by narrowing the letters at the sides of each line, to create the roundness of the bottle. It is interesting to speculate why some names were chosen rather than others, given that any town, city or county from 130 or more countries could have been chosen. To a certain extent, **phonological** (sound-related) factors will have been important: a Mexican name, such as 'Xochimilco', might have given English speakers some difficulty, and interrupted the fluency of their reading. But more important was probably the length of the name: all the names have between six and eight letters apiece. This enables a clear space to occur between each name and 'cream', enhancing the symmetry and smoothness of the shape created. At the same time, any place name with six to eight letters wouldn't do: consider the effect of 'Glasgow Cream' or 'Barnsley Cream', for example. These would be more likely to connote beer or hefty spirits than a genteel sherry – Harvey as the club bouncer rather than the cocktail party socialite.

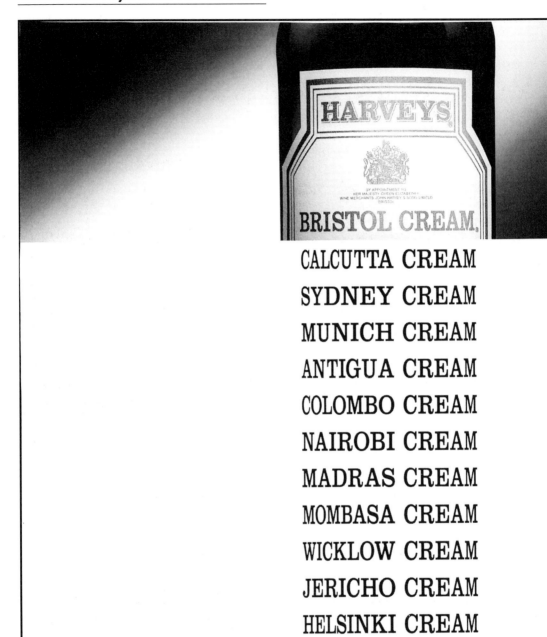

CALCUTTA CREAM
SYDNEY CREAM
MUNICH CREAM
ANTIGUA CREAM
COLOMBO CREAM
NAIROBI CREAM
MADRAS CREAM
MOMBASA CREAM
WICKLOW CREAM
JERICHO CREAM
HELSINKI CREAM
KINGSTON CREAM
PRAGUE CREAM
ST. LOUIS CREAM

Harveys is available in over 130 countries.

THE GUARDIAN Monday June 9 1986

Have you noticed how some people never like to say the word   ?

It's true   is a terrible disease, but it's not nearly as hopeless as it sounds.

In the past ten years enormous progress has been made in the treatment of   .

It is still, after road accidents, the major cause of death in children. But consider this.

Successful treatment of childhood   has risen from less than 10% in the 1950's to more than 50% today.

Many doctors are now convinced   will be the first cancer we will find a cure for.

With your help it will be.

Please give as much as you are able. Then by the year 2000, hopefully, people will no longer be scared to say the word   .

Because   will have disappeared forever.

Please send donations to the Leukaemia Research Fund, 43 Great Ormond Street, London WC1N3JJ. For credit card donations telephone 01-405 0101 and ask for Dept. GD.

In considering layouts and the other **graphological** devices (features associated with the visual aspects of texts), space is as important a consideration as verbal and non-verbal language. Empty spaces are as meaningful as filled ones. Where we expect language to occur, its non-occurrence is in itself an attention-seeking device.

Activity

Read Text: Charity appeal, which uses spaces to draw attention to public attitudes to

How far do you get before you are able to fill in the blanks as you read the advert?

When you have finished reading, try to pinpoint the strategies you used to help you work out what was missing.

Commentary

One strategy you may have employed is to look straight at the bottom of the page, to find the source of the text. Given that this is possible, it is interesting how many readers decide not to do this. Linguistic puzzles occur in many texts, from the crosswords and word-searches in adult newspapers and magazines to the code-breaking exercises in children's comics. This suggests that we find them pleasurable and interesting, and this is the reason perhaps why, despite the seriousness of the subject matter, some of us prefer to 'test' ourselves by trying to guess the blanks in this advert rather than looking straight at the answer.

The blank in the first line could be filled by a variety of different types of taboo word: for example, it could represent a swear word. However, by sentence 2 the choice has narrowed: it is defined as a disease. Its serious nature is suggested by the word 'terrible' in sentence 2 and the reference in sentence 4 to it as a major cause of death in children.

By sentence 6, we can define it further: a type of cancer.

The text itself never uses the word 'leukaemia', making it important for the reader to find the details at the bottom of the page in order to check the 'answer'. In so doing, the reader then registers the address for donations. The blank in the final line has extra resonance. Not only does it represent the non-appearance of the term 'leukaemia' in the same way as the other blanks in the text, it also represents the disappearance of the disease itself: the word and the referent have become one.

In making us work to fill in the blanks, not only does the text engage us, it also forces us to say the term 'leukaemia' over and over again. In reading the text and finding the answers, the reader is therefore unwittingly challenging the taboo that the advert is concerned with.

Space was used in the advert you have just been reading in order to foreground the idea of taboo and avoidance: the spaces mirror the fact that, so the text claims, the public suppress discussion of serious illness. The space is drawing attention to what should be present.

But space can refer to 'what should be present' in other ways, too. Because we know that advertising costs a lot of money, we expect advertisers to use up all their allotted space in order to get value for money. If they do not take this opportunity, we can perceive them to be self-effacing, not wishing to intrude upon our time and attention. In this case, texts can get attention by appearing to deny their own impact, and spaces can be read as a polite refusal to bully the reader.

Activity

Explain how Text: British Airways (1) uses notions of space to express ideas about its product and also about the audience it is addressing. There is no commentary here on this text, as it will be considered more fully in the next unit.

Extension

This unit has explored a variety of ways in which advertisements use attention-seeking devices. Here are some suggestions for taking these ideas further:

1   Collect some adverts which use startling *images* in order to get attention. Describe in detail how the images you have collected achieve their effect. Include consideration of the role of para-language, where appropriate. Also estimate the extent to which these images work in conjunction with any verbal text to convey messages.
2   Find some varied uses of graphological features (typographical variations and different layouts) in written advertising. Include consideration of the use of space as part of your exploration. What **connotations** (associations) and implied meanings are suggested by the features you have found?

23

This is for businessmen who don't have time to wait in check-in queues.

This is our Super Shuttle Executive self-service check-in machine.

TimeSaver for short.

It's a service you'll find at every Super Shuttle airport, giving frequent flyers the chance to by-pass the ticket and check-in desks altogether.

As you can see it works in much the same way as a bank cash dispenser. All you have to do is enter your TimeSaver card and select your destination and seat preference.

The machine will then charge the cost of your flight to your account (automatically giving you discount for off-peak travel) and give you your ticket and boarding pass.

All this takes less than a minute.

You can then proceed straight to the departure gate and catch your flight.

The perfect arrangement, we think, for the businessman or woman with precious little time to spare.

All we ask is that you be there at least ten minutes before take off.

If your flight happens to be full, you won't have to wait long for the next one either. We always have a back-up plane waiting in the wings.

And if you're in so much of a hurry to catch your flight that you don't have time to grab a bite to eat, we have some more good news for you.

Breakfast, lunch, tea, dinner or snacks are now served on all routes.

If you'd like to apply for a TimeSaver card, or any other information about Super Shuttle Executive, see your travel agent or your company travel coordinator.

Alternatively, you can call our TimeSaver information service on 0345 345757.

As soon as you have a moment, of course.

Super Shuttle Executive. Clearing your path from A to B.

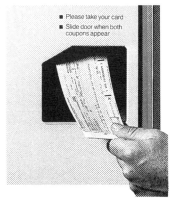

SUPER
SHUTTLE
EXECUTIVE

BRITISH AIRWAYS
The world's favourite airline.

This is for businessmen who don't even have time to read advertisements.

Call 0345 345757 for more information.

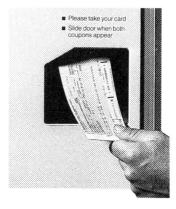

SUPER
SHUTTLE
EXECUTIVE

BRITISH AIRWAYS
The world's favourite airline.

25

3   Junk mailers often go to considerable lengths to get our attention – for example, by creating texts that masquerade as personal letters, postcards, 'prize draw winning' notices, and/or by getting the receiver to interact with it in some way, such as by cutting out elements, sticking stamps on particular squares, scratching off covers or undoing 'locked' parts with keys. Make a collection of junk mail by pooling the mail you get with that sent to other people you know. Classify some of their attention-seeking strategies: are some strategies more likely to be successful than others? To support your own assessments, conduct a survey to find out how people respond to the junk mail they receive.

three

Writers, readers and texts

Aim of this unit

In both earlier units, reference was made to the idea of the 'audience' for written advertisements. This unit looks more specifically at this idea.

There are many different terms for the people on either side of a text such as an advertisement. Here are some of them:

writer .... reader
sender .... receiver
producer .... consumer
addresser .... addressee

The reason why such terms have proliferated is that over the years there have been different models of this relationship, drawn from different academic domains, each of which has its own vocabulary to mirror the way it sees the world. For example, the terms 'writers and readers', from literary studies, suggest that the text should be seen primarily as an artistic written entity, composed by a creative individual; the phrase 'senders and receivers' calls up ideas of science, messages being seen as factual transmissions sent en masse via wires or through the air rather than on the page; 'producers and consumers', from the social sciences, emphasises the commercially driven nature of the interaction, text as trade; 'addresser and addressee', from linguistics, sees text as spoken interaction in face-to-face personal communication.

The term 'audience' itself suggests another kind of model. Originally, audience meant 'hearers', as in people who sit in a theatre 'auditorium' – the 'hearing area'. What was being heard (and seen) was a performance. So this pair of terms, 'performer (or actor) ...... audience' takes the model of dramatic performance as its framework for description.

It is not particularly useful to spend hours weighing up these different terms in order to arrive at the 'correct' one. What is important is to get a sense of why these different subject areas should think of advertising in a particular way, and to feel able to take helpful ideas from any or all of them. In fact, there is probably an element of 'truth' in each version: advertising often uses literary devices; it often uses aspects of scientific technology to carry its messages to a commercial marketplace for purposes of trade; adverts can employ a 'voice' which appears to be speaking personally to the reader; advertising texts can sometimes be considerably more dramatic than the programmes or articles they punctuate. In the end, it is beneficial rather than problematic that different subject areas want to say something about advertising, and that there are different models to draw from.

This unit and the next one will explore some analytical frameworks taken from literature and linguistics in order to look at the way advertising texts work as forms of discourse.

One aspect of literary study which can be useful when looking at written advertisements is the idea of the **narrator**, and **narrative point of view** within prose fiction. This is a good starting point for thinking about who is initiating the communication (i.e. the writer/sender/producer/addresser/performer side of the communication process).

WRITER AND NARRATOR

Literary criticism would make a sharp distinction between the writer of a text and the narrator of it. The writer is the person who constructs the text in reality; the narrator is the storyteller within the text – the person who appears to be addressing us, and guiding us through the narrative. This distinction can be illustrated by examples such as a female writer who constructs a male narrator, or an adult writer whose narrator is a child. The distinction enables us to identify the 'ownership' of the voice, and to think about the way the language of the text sets up this voice by a range of linguistic devices. In advertising texts, the real writers are the copywriters and artists who work in an advertising agency's creative department; but these people can construct all sorts of different narrators to convey to us the message of an advert - anything from a well-known actor to a cartoon figure, with a whole range of anonymous figures in between.

Another aspect of the split between the writer and narrator is the point of view that the narrator has in the story. The narrator might be a character in the story itself, and so addressing us in the **first person** - i.e. using the 'I' pronoun; or this narrator might be an observer of events, telling us about characters, actions and ideas by using 'he', 'she', 'it' and 'they', in which case the narrator would be said to be using **third person** address. These choices may appear to represent small changes, but they can produce some powerfully different effects.

Activity

To explore the ideas presented above, look back at the NSPCC and Leukaemia Research adverts you studied previously. Both texts use 'third person' address, describing situations as if from a detached point of view: for example, 'This child is three months old . . .' (NSPCC); '. . . in the past ten years enormous progress has been made . . .' (Leukaemia Research). As a result, the narrators of the texts appear as independent observers and commentators on the work of the charities.

Choose one of these texts, and change the address term into a form of first-person narrative (i.e. using either 'I' or 'we'). You will probably need to recast whole sections of text for this, rather than simply change pronouns and leave everything else the same.

If you would prefer to start from scratch, then think of a charity you could write some material for, and write an advert which encourages readers to make donations. Write your text in the first person.

When you have finished, compare your own texts with the NSPCC and Leukaemia Research adverts. What different effects have arisen from the various address forms used?

Commentary

In comparing your own texts with the NSPCC and Leukaemia Research adverts, you may have found the following:

Use of 'we'

Liberal use of this pronoun to address the reader may have the effect of making the charity sound like a commercial organisation. It will certainly sound authoritarian – 'we are the authors of this text, we have opinions and we are telling you what they are'.

'We' can have connotations of territoriality and group definition – corporate ownership. This is not an image that a charity would want to project. Interestingly, the Leukaemia text does use 'we' once, but this connects more with 'many doctors' or the idea of 'society in general' than with the charity specifically.

Use of 'I'

This may sound overly personal, too individualised to represent a charitable group. If you used 'I' as the voice of a 'character' (for example, the voice of the child in the NSPCC advert) this could sound manipulative – deliberately sentimental and rather mawkish. We know that the child could not really address us, so the advert's strategies would be laid bare. Also, it might appear that we were dealing with an individual, one-off case of cruelty and, as a consequence, the effect of an independent observer recounting what is all too common an event would be lost.

NARRATEE

Literary criticism can also offer some ideas on the other aspect of the address context - the reader/receiver/consumer/addressee/audience part of the communication process. Just as it is useful to make a distinction between the writer and narrator of a text, so it is important to think about differences between real readers and the readers that are implied by the text. Advertisements, like literary texts, are not aimed at a single private reader in the way, for example, a personal letter is. On the other hand, they are certainly not completely aimless, without a notion of audience. In the end, we need to look at the way the text is constructed in order to gather clues about who is the main address target. If we call the constructed persona who appears to be talking the 'narrator', we can call the people who appear to be being addressed **narratees**. These people might be specifically addressed, as in the address to 'Tobacconists' in the Tobacco Advisory Council advert in Unit 1; or they might be a much less specific group, defined less by explicit name and more by the qualities and values they are thought to possess. There can be more than one narrator, and more than one group of narratees. In the Tobacco Advisory Council text, for example, we saw that there were several sets of people 'talking' to each other in and via the advert.

The widest address forms to be given to a narratee in an advertisement are no address form at all (0) or 'you'. In both these cases, any person reading the advert can feel addressed by it and not excluded from the communication. Both the charity adverts you studied previously use the word 'you' (or the possessive form, 'your') to address the reader. In both cases, this word is used at the point where the reader is asked to act:

> To provide care and protection for one child costs £15.40 a week. *You* can help by sending all or part of that sum, using the coupon below.
>
> (NSPCC)

> Many doctors are now convinced   will be the first cancer we will find a cure for. With *your* help it will be. Please give as much as *you* are able.
>
> (Leukaemia Research)

There is no clear identifiable group being named, as would be the case if the advert in question had said 'All you people who earn more than X amount per year', and yet there is a sense that the reader should be a certain kind of person, should want to behave in a certain way. In wanting to be a certain kind of person as we read and interact with the text, we become narratees – in other words, we position ourselves in the way the text wants us to.

The general public – the 'real readers' – are composed of all kinds of people, not all of whom would, presumably, care about the causes that are being described in these texts, nor would they be persuaded by the cases and arguments being presented.

But the real readers are addressed as if they are caring people who, although they may not make any contributions to charities at the moment, have the potential to do so – hence the coupon in the NSPCC advert, and the address for donations in the Leukaemia text. The Leukaemia text also tells us we are different from the 'some people' at the start, who are too frightened to mention you-know-what. In reality, we might be the very people the text is talking about, but we are encouraged to think we are superior to those people: we are brave enough to confront this cancer and reduce its power by both naming it and funding the scientific research that may be able to eradicate it. Both these charity adverts, then, give real readers the sense that they could be the people they would like to be.

To summarise: even though advertisements might not explicitly name their narratees, they are likely to indicate a ' kind of person', a profile that is presumed to exist. This kind of person may not match the real readers of the texts; but he or she might be someone that the real readers would like to be, would like to aspire to. In identifying themselves with this profile, readers 'become' the narratees of the text.

More pragmatically, advertisements are often placed in publications where it is thought readers will be likely to identify themselves with the profile in the text. The Leukaemia Research advert, for example, appeared in the *Guardian*, whose readers are likely to think of themselves as people who would support charitable causes, even though they might not do anything practical about that desire at present. It would be wasteful for any advert to talk to large groups of real readers who are not going to see themselves as its narratees.

Activity

It is probably easier to examine the complex ideas above where the narratees are more explicitly defined. Go back to the British Airways advert at the end of Unit 2 and read this text again.

Commentary

This advert announces explicitly who it thinks it is talking to. It names two types of narratee, in the following ways:

This is for businessmen who don't have time to wait in check-in queues.

This is for businessmen who don't even have time to read advertisements.

In the text on the left, the narrator refers to himself as 'we', which we take to be the voice of BA, the company whose logo appears at the bottom of the advert. The narratee is addressed as 'you' throughout the text, yet we know who the 'you' is, through the use of the term 'businessmen' in the hookline (the enlarged text at the top), and through the image of the male hand extending from the business suit and shirt cuff. This figure – the narratee – is defined as an incredibly busy person whose valuable time must not be wasted in trivial ways, such as in queuing for tickets.

But there is an even busier businessman than the one on the left: the one on the right doesn't even have time to read adverts. The text on the right humbly deletes itself accordingly, visually enacting what the Super Shuttle Executive Service claims to be about: 'Clearing your path from A to B'. The advert strips itself down to its bare essentials in order not to make demands on this impossibly busy narratee. There is a relationship here between the two narratees on either side of the text, in that the one on the left would presumably like to think of himself as the one on the right – a man in an ultimate hurry, intent on matters of utmost importance. You could argue that the narratee on the right is the 'real' one, the real image to aspire to, defined through rejection of the less busy figure on the left.

But what about the ordinary readers of this text – the readers who are not businessmen hurtling around the globe? For us, the message is a different one. We know we are not being addressed by this advert, but we are its viewers too. In a sense, we are onlookers to the scene. The message for us is that there are important people around who are being offered the privilege to queue-jump because their work is high-powered stuff and because they can afford to pay for a special service.

Activity

Text: British Airways (2) is another BA advert.
 Read it through and decide the following:

◎ Why does the narrator switch into another language halfway through the advert, and what effect does this have?
◎ Who is the narratee for this text?
◎ What do you think is the role of the readers who are not specifically being addressed by the advert?

(Note: there is no commentary on this text.)

While other people are reading their morning paper at Heathrow können Sie die Zeitung in Hamburg lesen.

British Airways news for businessmen is that we have more early flights each day to more European cities than any other airline.

BRITISH AIRWAYS
The world's favourite airline.

Extension

This unit has focused on the way in which an advertisement can establish point of view as a result of the way the language of the text constructs narrators and narratees.

To explore this idea further, collect some adverts that seem to you to have an identifiable narrative voice, and explain how that voice is constructed from the language used. Also look for the ways in which some adverts appear to make assumptions about who is being addressed and, again, explain how the language gives rise to those assumptions. You are likely to find that the two areas above – that of the narrative voice, and that of the narratee(s) – are strongly connected in any one particular text, but it may be helpful for you to concentrate on one aspect at a time in order to build up your analysis.

Unit four

How does that sound?

Aim of this unit

In the previous unit, the word 'voice' was used at some points, to describe the way in which the narrator addressed the narratee. This word calls up ideas of spoken language rather than written, and it is the area of spoken language that this unit will explore. The overall aim is to enable you to see how written adverts, despite being page-bound, often use aspects of spoken language in order to achieve their effects. In order to appreciate this, some detailed work on the nature of speech will be necessary.

It is difficult for us to answer the question 'What is real speech like?' for a number of reasons. One is its transient nature: up to now, it has not been an easy task for us to preserve it for study. To be able to study it in a controlled way is important, because it is such an integral part of our daily behaviour that it is quite hard for us to stand back from it and analyse it. However, our ability to study speech is now changing as a result of new technologies: for example, computer corpuses can provide us with accurate recordings and transcriptions of millions of spoken words, collected from many different types of interaction. It is only by finding repeated patterns that we can really say how spoken language 'works'.

Speech has a lot of catching up to do. For several centuries, all our archives that tell us about language have been based on writing, and recorded in writing. Writing has such high status that we tend to think all its representations are accurate, even when writing has the cheek to impersonate speech – a medium clearly not designed for the page.

The aim of the work that follows is to help you sort out how real speech differs from the way it often appears in constructed texts, such as literary fiction; at the same time, it will be important to notice which features literary writers choose to represent, as well as to ignore. Writers need to give us a sense that their characters could exist, so in choosing aspects of speech to represent, they must choose some aspects that we recognise intuitively. This work will be the starting point for thinking about further types of written texts that use aspects of speech to give themselves more communicative force.

Activity

Text 1: Fictive dialogue is an extract from the novel *Union Street*, by Pat Barker. The extract depicts an incident in a factory on Tyneside, where one of the female employees is physically attacking another by chopping at her hair with scissors. How does the writer attempt to suggest some aspects of spoken language in this scene?

(For a commentary on this activity, see the commentary after Text 2: Real speech.)

Text 1: Fictive dialogue

Lilian's failure to stand up for herself took away what little self-control Elaine had. She stabbed at the hair, sawing and hacking away almost at random.

'There you are. Give that lot a bit trim and you'll be all right.'

Elaine's voice shook with laughter. 'No, hold on, there's a bit here.'

Elaine nearly choked. 'I'll finish it off.'

'What about the top, Elaine?' Giggle suggested.

'I think it's gone far enough,' Jo said.

Elaine stopped what she was doing and looked at Jo.

'What's it to do with you?'

'Nowt. But I think it's gone far enough. Don't you?'

'You want to make something of it?'

'No. But I will if I have to.'

Elaine looked around for support. There was none. Some of the older women at the head of the table were getting reluctantly to their feet.

'She's better off without it.'

'I'm not denying that. But you might've let her make up her own mind.'

'*Mind?* She hasn't got a bloody mind!'

'No reason to pick on her. We all know what's eating you. If you haven't got the guts to speak out you'd best shut up altogether.'

'Come on girls. Come on'. It was the manager. He stood in the open doorway, angrily consulting his watch. 'These tea breaks are meant to be fifteen minutes, you know. Fifteen. Not thirty.'

He watched them file past. Looking for trouble, he noticed one of the girls walking along without a hairnet on.

'You,' he said. 'Whatever your name is.'

'Lil-.'

He wasn't interested. 'Get your hair under that net. And don't ever let me catch you walking round like that again.'

Activity

Having thought about the literary extract, now look at Text 2, a transcript of some real speech. The speakers are two women who know each other well. A has invited B round to her house to go for a walk. B arrives on her bicycle at the front door, then takes her bike round to the back and takes it into the house.

The transcript has been simplified in various ways, showing only where simultaneous speech occurs (segments marked with asterisks) and how the speech is broken up into intonation units (segments marked with dashes). No attempt has been made to indicate the types of tune being used, but syllables marked by particular stress have been shown by capitals.

Note also that the following, which were present in the real voice production, have not been marked here: volume, speed, pitch range, voice tension or laxity, pauses.

Compare this piece of real speech with the literary representation you studied earlier. What aspects of spoken language are present in the real speech, but ignored or present less often in the fictional version? Why do any such differences exist, do you think?

Text 2: Real speech

(A greets B at the front door.)
A: HIya - got the back GATE *open*
B: *RIGHT*
(A meets B at the back door.)
A: what a BRILLiant day - put it in HERE - AYE - get IN there love
B: oh AYE - alRIGHT - it was aMAZing coming over the TOPS - over just up - over by *Stalybridge*
A: *mm*
B: but my BIKE'S - a bit of a STATE *and*
A: *WHY* - it looks alRIGHT
B: it's NOT - it's - it needs a SERvice - but I haven't got time and *(trailing off)*
A: oh yeah - well
B: STUpid - I mean - it's my main transport - and I get really worked *UP*
A: *put* it along HERE
B: I've brought you some CHOICE PRODuce - from the allotment - uh - jerusalem artichokes
A: oh EXCellent - what do you DO with them
B: well - Jeanette does this BRILLiant soup - where you SCRUB them - and BOIL them - till they go sort of MUSHy - then you get some BUTter - and fry smokey BACon - and ONions - and all stuff like THAT - and put them INTO it - with uh - with some - what ELSE does she put in it - yeah - STOCK - stock and more BUTter - and CREAM - and put it all in the BLENder - it's really *GORgeous*
A: *mm*
B: but they're very FARTy - and Jeanette says this recipe is FART proof *(laughter)*
A: RIGHT - so
B: so where we GOING then
A: I thought we could do THIS - the Tintwistle CIRcular - cos I've never DONE it *and*
B: *BRILL*
A: we could end UP there - for a tiny PINT
B: YES - a TIny TIny PINT - oh YES

Para language

The real speech situation is firmly embedded in its immediate surroundings. This means that a great deal of meaning can be conveyed by the physical aspects of communication, such as gesture, body posture and eye contact. This was referred to earlier as 'paralanguage', which also includes the tone of voice and spasmodic effects produced by a speaker – such as laughter, breathiness and whispering.

Note that, while in real speech all these aspects would have been present and meaningful (and at some points have been marked in order to help the reading of the data), the literary version has to be explicit in describing what is going on: for example, actions such as 'She stabbed at the hair', 'Elaine stopped what she was doing and looked at Jo', 'Elaine looked around for support', 'the older women at the head of the table were getting reluctantly to their feet', 'He watched them file past'; and speech effects such as 'Elaine's voice shook with laughter', 'Elaine nearly choked'.

Deictics

Also because of its context dependency, real speech often makes use of what are termed **deictics** – reference terms such as 'this', 'that', 'those', 'it', 'here' and 'there', which indicate items in the immediate context. For example, in Text 2 speaker A says, of B's bicycle, 'put it in here' and 'put it along here'. The utterance doesn't need to be any more specific than that, as both speakers know that 'it' is the bicycle and 'here' refers to a particular place they can both see. Speaker A also says 'I thought we could do this', pointing to a page in a walker's guide book. The literary version also uses deictics, but it has to make sure that the reader already has a clear picture of what is being referred to. For example, the underlined deictics in the following section all refer back to the description of the attack on the hair in the first sentence:

She stabbed at the hair, sawing and hacking away almost at random.

'There you are. Give *that lot* a bit trim and you'll be all right.'

Elaine's voice shook with laughter. 'No, hold on, there's a bit *here*.'

Ellipsis

The way deictics often work in real speech is as a kind of shorthand: we don't need to spell everything out, because our interlocutor is with us in a shared physical context. **Ellipsis**, where elements of language are left out altogether, could be seen as another form of shorthand. This can often be as much to do with a shared emotional or attitudinal context as with a physical one: people who know each other well don't need to be all that explicit about their meanings, because they know the other person will fill in the gaps as a result of shared knowledge and shared history. An example of ellipsis in Text 2 is the word 'stupid': the full form of this would be something like 'the situation I'm referring to is really stupid'. If this conversation had been between people who didn't know each other very well, the full form of this utterance would have had to be used: the listener would then know that the word wasn't a reference to himself or herself.

Prosodic features

Both the texts represent **prosodic features** – aspects of spoken language such as intonation and stress, which are part of the overall 'melody' of a language. The difference is that in the real dialogue, these aspects were part of the general communicative force of the original interaction. In writing up the transcript, the transcriber has made some attempt to represent these features by specific markings.

The conversation in the literary text, of course, never took place, but it is in the interest of the writer to make the reader bring it to life as if it did. To this end, the literary writer uses typographical presentation, such as different typefaces and features of punctuation – here, the use of italics to signal stress, and question and exclamation marks to suggest the respective intonation patterns. These features present the spoken voice in a very impressionistic way: in other words, the literary writer uses a small range of written conventions, knowing that readers will read the cues and work to 'create' features of spoken dialogue inside their heads as they read.

Lexis

The **lexis** (vocabulary) of the two texts demonstrates some interesting differences and similarities. Both the real dialogue and the literary one use everyday, ordinary language. Pat Barker also makes some attempt to suggest regional language: 'a bit trim' instead of 'a bit of a trim'; 'nowt' instead of 'nothing'; 'hod' instead of 'hold', to indicate accent. Text 2 would, of course, have had features of accent, but the only way we could learn about this in looking at the text on the page would be to represent the language phonetically (i.e., using a sound alphabet). In fact, both speakers play around with accent, varying their strength of accent (speaker B lives in Manchester, A in Derbyshire) for comic purposes, and using regional dialect terms – 'aye', 'love' – in humorous role-play. Similar play can be seen in the self-conscious formality of 'choice produce' and 'excellent'. At the lexical level, speakers in both texts use reference to taboo to express attitude – in Text 1 a swear word expresses strength of feeling, while in Text 2 euphemistic expressions 'a tiny pint', 'a tiny tiny pint' are used ironically, as a humorous reference to the speakers' interest in drinking beer – not a habit traditionally approved of for women. Discussion of the fart-inducing nature of artichokes also produces laughter.

The literary extract doesn't simply have dialogue, though: it also has a narrator telling us what's going on in terms both of external action and of the inside of the character's heads (third-person narrator). We understand that this is a different 'voice', partly because of the lack of speech marks, but also because the style is subtly different: the lexis tends to be more abstract and more formal – for example, 'failure', 'self-control', 'consult'.

Repetition

The real data involves more repetition, both lexically and **grammatically**, than the constructed version. In real speech, we tolerate repetition, or perhaps even expect and need it, as a support to our memories. In writing, we expect variation of structures, which we see as a part of stylistic elegance. The issue of burdening the memory is not a problem: if we get lost in reading written text, we can go back and start again. You could say, then, that a literary writer's conventions for constructing dialogue in some ways owe more to writing than to spoken language.

One way in which this can be seen very clearly is in speaker B's extensive use of the connective 'and' in Text 2. Such co-ordination is the norm for speech, particularly in storytelling episodes, but extensive use of 'and' is considered poor style in writing, and tends to be used in literary constructions to characterise a child speaker. This is different from a single instance of 'and' at the beginning of a sentence or utterance, which can signal dramatic emphasis, as in Text 1:

> 'Get your hair under that net. And don't ever let me catch you walking round like that again.'

Non-fluency features

Further differences between the two texts include what are often called normal **non-fluency features** (Crystal and Davy 1969) – hesitations, fillers, false starts, changing course in mid-utterance and incompleteness. In everyday discourse we consider such features to be a normal part of interactions, yet they rarely appear in constructed versions of speech, and they would be completely absent in writing which is not trying to represent spoken language.

Our different rules about what constitutes fluency often lead to different grammatical sequences in speech and writing: for example, full sentences, the norm for writing, are rarer in speech. Consider the utterances 'got the back gate open' and 'where we going then' in Text 2. The full versions of these would be 'I've got the back gate open' and 'where are we going then'. In Text 1, the dialogue overwhelmingly uses complete, full sentences, even though the characters are in a tense situation where such explicit language would actually be unlikely.

Interaction markers

Similar disparities occur in what might be termed **interaction markers**, which are those aspects of language that result from speech as a co-operative activity involving **turn-taking** – features such as overlaps and interruptions, reinforcements (encouraging 'noises' such as 'mm' and 'yeah') and monitoring expressions such as 'you know?' where the speaker checks out with the listener that they understand and are still paying attention. Interaction markers are noticeably lacking in the literary version, even though the emotions of the speakers would be likely to trigger many more interruptions and overlaps than in Text 2. There is one interruption in Text 1, which is read as a signal that the manager wants to exert his power.

Topic changes

The texts also differ markedly in the way **topic changes** work within the interactions. In literary texts, dialogue exists to elaborate characters and dramatise events. As a result, interactions tend to stay on one topic or theme for a considerable length of time, even though there may, as here, be a fast pace of turn-taking. But compare the number of topics dealt with in Text 1 and Text 2. In the latter, much more characteristic of real interactions, we have the following, through which the speakers weave humour and references to shared ideas as a part of their continuing relationship:

greetings
directions
comments on the weather/scenery
the condition of the bike
the problem of getting the bike serviced
the present of artichokes
a recipe
a caution
planning a walk
planning an evening drink.

Summary

Constructed speech in literary texts chooses to imitate some aspects of real speech but to leave other aspects out. We have been looking at a piece of literature which was consciously trying to suggest the voices of working-class, regionally accented female speakers engaged in a heated confrontation. It is important to realise that different pieces of literature (and different parts of the same literary text) might have different concerns and interests. For example, to suggest the voice of a middle-class male politician delivering a speech would require a particular kind of presentation which would differ markedly from the extract you have just read.

Given the difficulty with large generalisations it is, however, still valid to summarise some of the findings that have emerged so far from the data studied.

The literary dialogue can be profiled as follows, in terms of the features present and absent:

◎ Prosody: some aspects represented (e.g. intonation, stress) by italics and punctuation marks.
◎ Accent: represented very minimally, by alteration of one spelling.
◎ Vocabulary: chosen to indicate 'everyday conversation' and region of speakers. But no suggestion of the level of repetition found in real data.
◎ Grammar: one piece of dialect grammar to suggest region. But literary version mainly has full sentences and explicit structures that resemble writing rather than speech. No use of ellipsis; some use of deictics, but these have to be fully supported in the narrator's part of the text.

◎ Interaction markers: one example of an interruption. No sense of the range of features present in speech.
◎ Fluency: no normal 'non-fluency' features.
◎ Paralanguage: has to be independently described by narrator.
◎ Topic changes: nothing like the frequency and variation seen in real speech.

We will be returning to this list when we look at some adverts that use aspects of spoken language.

FUNCTIONS

So far, the emphasis has been on the **features** of spoken language; but speech also differs considerably from writing in its **functions.** While looking at features can tell us about the structure of language, consideration of function relates more to what we do with it: for example, why we might choose to speak rather than write, the qualities speech and writing are thought to communicate, and how we feel about the two codes. Feelings are crucial where advertising is concerned because as a form of communication it consciously targets our emotions.

Activity

The next two texts are two versions of a recipe. The first, Text: Spoken recipe, is a spoken version accompanying a cookery demonstration, from a television programme concerning food and drink; the second, Text: Ceefax recipe, is the written version that appeared that same evening on Ceefax.

Both pieces of material are extracts, since the originals, particularly the spoken one, would be too long to include intact. In their full forms, the spoken transcript would have taken up four times more space on the page than the written text. This simple fact already tells us a lot about the functional differences between speech and writing: speech is a speedy medium where you can cover a lot of ground in a short time.

Read through the two extracts and this time, as well as concentrating on the features that differ, think about the purposes of the two texts and what they communicate:

◎ Do we use the texts for the same purposes – are they doing the same things?

◎　Do they communicate the same ideas and information, the same attitudes and feelings?

◎　Do you feel more positive about one rather than the other? If so, why do you think that is?

The chef in the spoken extract is called Alan Herriot. The programme's presenter is John Forfar, and his introductory remarks are given here, to show how the programme 'set the scene' for the cookery feature. (Note: no attempt has been made here to indicate prosodic features.)

Text: Spoken recipe

JF: hello and welcome to another feast of information and temptation with food and drink in which Alan Herriot takes wing

AH: well actually it's more like a flight of fancy it's going to be a duck recipe duck breasts just searing two wild duck breasts in there to serve with a lovely Chinese set of flavours and a wild rice pilau speaking of wild

(The camera pans to the two drinks experts, for their introduction to the drink features coming up in the rest of the programme. After that, the programme presents a number of documentary-style features on aspects of food, before returning to the studio for the cookery item.)

AH: I've been cooking these duck breasts for a little while now in fact you can use domestic or wild duck like barbary or campbell khaki a wonderful name for duck I'm going to start adding flavours ginger first now you can this is crushed fresh ginger I've taken it from the root and peeled and crushed it but you can buy jars of it ready crushed which are hugely useful and valuable if you're in a bit of a hurry about an ounce or so of ginger a couple of big tablespoons if you're using the crushed version and then a little water just a wine glass of water and a quick stir so that the flavours of the ginger and the duck start to mingle now that needs to simmer for about ten minutes until the duck's almost cooked through and meanwhile you can be starting the pilau the delicious wild rice dish that goes with this

Text: Ceefax recipe

Chinese style duck with pilau rice

Ingredients
(for 2 persons)
2 duck breasts
1oz root ginger, peeled and crushed
4 tbsp water

Method
1   Heat a heavy-based frying pan and cook the duck breasts, skin side down, for five minutes over a medium heat. Do not add oil, or the breasts will produce a surprising amount of fat.
2   Pour most of the fat out of the pan and discard. Turn the breasts over, add the root ginger and the water. Cook for about 10 minutes until the water has evaporated and the duck is cooked through.

Commentary

Although the two texts are both concerned with how to cook a particular recipe, they serve different purposes as pieces of communication. The spoken text is embedded in action, and is part of a performance, while the written text is much more concerned with information, consisting of a list followed by clearly demarcated instructions. As a result of this basic difference, the spoken text feels much more personal, while the written one feels colder and more impersonal – although the word 'surprising' in the written version does suggest an emotional quality, in that it describes an internal state of mind rather than an external action.

The sense of human agency in the spoken text derives from many sources: for example, the speaker's use of 'I' and 'you' to describe the people who are involved in the communication; the speaker's expression of his personal feelings, as in his description of the names of ducks, and in his many sensual adjectives such as 'lovely' and 'delicious'; the speaker's characterisation of the lives of his listeners as busy people who might see the value of ready-crushed ginger; the speaker's determination not to be too precise or scientific sounding, as in 'I've been cooking these duck breasts for a little while now', 'an ounce or so', and 'a couple of big tablespoons'.

Such overt expressions of relationship between chef and audience (or 'narrator' and 'narratee', if we adopt the terms used in the previous unit) are noticeably lacking in the written version. Moreover, the written text has to be explicit about aspects that are physically present in the speech context – apparently mundane factors such as the heavy-based frying pan, cooking the duck breasts skin side down, and the lack of oil. Such details make the written version sound much more factual, concerned with 'the basics' rather than any subtlety. This is compounded by the lack of subtlety in the term 'cook', which is used twice in the written version, as opposed to 'sear' and 'simmer' in the spoken one; and by the scientific-sounding 'until the water has evaporated' compared with the sensuous description in the spoken text of the mingling of flavours.

VARIETIES OF SPEECH AND WRITING

The material we have just been studying showed a marked difference between the spoken and written data. The spoken data expressed human agency and, as a result, conveyed a sense of personal relationship between speaker and listener (or narrator and narratee), while the written text, in contrast, appeared more impersonal, less expressive emotionally and less individualised.

We tend to use writing where we want the ability to be at one remove from our audience, and where we want the opportunity to be controlled and well prepared. On the other hand, where we want expressive spontaneity, spoken face-to-face communication is likely to be favoured.

But there is no simple binary of speech versus writing. What we have in reality is a continuum of forms where varieties of speech and writing are more or less controlled and consciously pre-planned:

more-planned writing	academic essays, legal forms
less-planned writing	personal letters, e-mail
less-planned speech	informal conversation
more-planned speech	political speeches, scripted performance

In fact, there are many overlaps in the middle of this diagram, with some types of informal writing demonstrating features that we might associate with informal chat. For example, Text: E-mail is an e-mail message sent by one family member to another (let's call the writer A and the reader B). Although this is writing, you have here the kind of rapid topic change that we observed in the informal dialogue on p. 40, as well as many examples of ellipsis that relate to the shared understanding of A and B, both in the wide sense of a knowledge of family circumstances, and in the narrower sense of the communication that went directly before.

Activity

Read Text: E-mail through carefully, and try to ascertain the following:

◎   What details of family circumstances are already shared by A and B?
◎   What can you infer from this text about the e-mail sent previously by B to A?
◎   What new information is being presented here for B?

Text: E-mail

Hiya, haven't been around much lately as I've been working solid up until today. I wondered if you had had bad weather and was going to contact you tonight anyway. All we've had so far are frosty nights and wet and windy days. I've now been put on a permanent shift at work with Gerry, who is also an ex-policeman, and he knows all the people I know so we get on really well. I'm working days up to Xmas including Xmas eve, then have 8 days off. I'll get everyone to send you vouchers then if that makes it easier. How's the car going? I've just had to spend £400 on the Volvo! New rear box, pipe and pinion seal. Hope I haven't bought a lemon! Val says she doesn't know how she ever managed without the kitchen tongs you sent her. It's the baby's christening Sunday and we're looking for a bonnet but can't find one. I called in there today and she's three months old now, and laughing at me. Si is still doing well at work, and has been the only technician on the premises while his boss has been in Florida.

Keep warm then, I'll let you know how everything went after the weekend.

Love from the soggy South. xxx

Shared (or 'given') information

A and B appear to share knowledge of family members, whose names need no explanation: for example 'Val', 'Si'; there is also understanding of what is meant by 'everyone'. The phrase 'the baby' implies no name is needed, as there is only one person whom that label could describe (either through there being no other babies in the family, or through its recent arrival). It is interesting that the baby is about to be christened. Perhaps this is the rite of passage at which point she acquires a real 'name'.

Cars owned by A and B are known. There is also reference, perhaps previously established, to geographical location – the 'South'.

There is a sense of shared meaning at an emotional level. For example, A communicates that he is happy at work, that Val is pleased with her present, that the baby is laughing and that Si is doing well; A is secure enough to admit his own worry that he might have bought a dud car; the e-mail ends affectionately. All these aspects demonstrate A's selection of detail to construct a positive communication for B, and assume B's emotional engagement and interest in the details of family members' lives.

There are also examples of given information which appear to relate less to the permanently shared set of meanings about family circumstances, and more to B's previous communication: for example, both the initial comments about the weather B had experienced and the reference to vouchers appear as responses to previous and specific communication by B on these topics.

New information

Although knowledge of the people referred to in A's communication is shared, some aspects of their lives are presented as new information: for example, that Val is grateful for the kitchen tongs and uses them a lot, that Si is being given responsibility at work, that the baby is about to be christened. There is a similar pattern with the car theme: while A's car is known, its ailments are new information.

Details of the weather, of days off, and of the intention to contact B are all new, as is the information about the existence of A's workmate, Gerry.

This activity should have demonstrated the extent to which informal writing between friends can share the characteristics of informal dialogue, particularly in its ability not to have to set everything out explicitly, but to be able to trade on shared references. You could say that writing of this type, like informal speech, exists in the form it does because we know we are supposed to 'read between the lines' as we go – registering the information already shared ('given information'), and paying particular attention to new aspects ('new information').

PRESUPPOSITION

In an area of linguistics which has developed theoretical frameworks for how we 'make sense' of interactions (called **Speech Act Theory**) 'given' information is termed **presupposition** (ideas taken for granted), and it is often suggested that many of our meanings are encoded at this level. Speech act theorists would claim that presupposition is a necessary aspect of conversation, because it makes for economy, without which interactions would be hopelessly long-winded. For example, the question below, asked of someone in a pub:

Have you got a light, please?

contains several presuppositions, as follows:

◎   that 'light' is understood as match or other incendiary device for lighting cigarettes
◎   that 'light' is understood as the above in working order (the speaker would not be pleased to be offered a lighter which had run out of fuel, where the owner knew it wasn't working)
◎   that if the person addressed does have a functioning 'light', s/he will do more than simply say so: the question requires more than a 'yes/no' answer.

Imagine how tedious conversation would be if, instead of the question above, you had to say the following:

Are you in possession of a box of matches or cigarette lighter, please, and, if you are, are they in working order, and would you be willing to allow me to use either of them, and could you therefore indicate that willingness or otherwise by responding?

If the utterance above is reminiscent of Star Trek's Mr Spock, this is not coincidental: one of the ways the programme demonstrated this character's non-humanness was by his over-explicit use of language, to signal a 'logical' mind, in contrast to the 'intuitive' shared meanings communicated by the human beings. This should be a reminder to us of the culture-specific nature of language: a human's presupposition could therefore be completely baffling to a Vulcan, and vice versa.

USER FRIENDLINESS

The e-mail text considered previously was a piece of informal writing between relatives, and we observed that it shared characteristics with informal dialogue, particularly in terms of rapid topic changes and presuppositional meanings. But other types of writing which are more in the public domain, such as commercially produced non-fiction books, can also try to call up the spoken voice. This is sometimes what we are noticing when we say a text is 'user friendly'.

Activity

In Text: Delia Smith recipes are brief extracts from the beginnings of three Delia Smith recipes. Compare these extracts with the Ceefax written recipe studied earlier: how does Delia Smith's writing draw on spoken language? What effects are produced?

In analysing the data, don't forget to think about any relevant aspects of the textual features considered in Units 1–3 and in the earlier part of this unit.

(Note: (1) the typeface variations below mirror those in the original text; (2) there is no commentary on this activity.)

Text: Delia Smith recipes

Perfect Roast Potatoes
Serves 8
The amounts here are not vital because it depends on who's greedy and who is on a diet and so on, but I find that 8oz (225g) per person is enough - yielding three each and a few extras for inevitable second helpings!

> ### Four Nut Chocolate Brownies
> If you've never made brownies before, you first need to get into the brownie mode, and to do this stop thinking 'cakes'. Brownies are slightly crisp on the outside but soft, damp and squidgey within. I'm always getting letters from people who think their brownies are not cooked, so once you've accepted the description above, try and forget all about cakes.
>
> ### Cranberry and Orange One-Crust Pies
> Serves 6
> I seem to have a craze at the moment for cooking everything in individual portions. I love individual steamed puddings and now I'm into making individual pies as well. These are dead simple to make, easy to serve and the rich, luscious flavour of the cranberries is extremely good.

Cookery books, although basically informative, are adverts in a way: they are selling us the idea of cooking the dishes they feature, and in so doing, the books are selling themselves as necessary tools, as instruction manuals, as 'how-to' texts. It is important that we have confidence in the writer as a good teacher, and one way we may feel confident about a teacher is if they 'speak our language', if they are 'on our wavelength'. To achieve this, it is important for the writer not to seem too remote and authoritarian, but rather to be a friend who just happens to be an expert. Using aspects of language that we associate with spoken interactions can help construct exactly that kind of profile for the writer.

Activity

'A friend who is an expert' is not a bad profile for the narrator in an advert to have, either. Text: Banking Direct is an advert from the Bank of Scotland's Banking Direct division, selling loans. It arrived as what we now call 'junk mail' – unsolicited material which arrives on the doormat, along with our personal letters. The advert is written as a personal letter, but as if it were a spoken interaction between two people – someone from the company, and the person to whom the letter is addressed.

How does the advert use ideas about how spoken language works?

BANK OF SCOTLAND
BANKING DIRECT

Banking Direct, Teviot House, 41 South Gyle Crescent, Edinburgh EH12 9DR

Ms A Goddard

Ref: G10
September 1996

Dear Ms Goddard

What did you think of our letter?

What letter?

The letter we wrote to you in July. The one about the privileged loan with interest rates from only 13.9% APR, for a loan of £3,000 or more over 36 months.

O.K. but what's the catch?

No catch, this is a great offer. Why not call our friendly staff on 0800 805 805 and set up that loan for those home improvements, or holiday you've been planning.

Also, with a *Deferred Payment Option*, you can enjoy the benefits of a preferential rate personal loan (typical APRs are just 13.9% for a loan of £3,000 over 36 months), without a penny to pay until 3 months from the day the loan begins.

I know, but I'm too busy. I can never find the time.

We understand but a few minutes are all you need. We're here 24 hours a day, 7 days a week. Our friendly staff will take your details and give you a decision in minutes. Just call.

How do I know this is a good offer?

Just take a look at the rates available from some other high street lenders and you'll see Bank of Scotland offers excellent value for money.

0800 805 805

0004530/0393738/20361   Head Office: The Mound, Edinburgh EH1 1YZ   29421AV2

G10

INTEREST RATE COMPARISONS						
	APR (without Deferred Payment Option)	Total Number of Repayments	Monthly Repayment	Total Amount Payable	Savings if loan taken with Bank of Scotland	Fixed Penalty for early repayment of loan
Bank of Scotland	13.9%	36	£101.33	£3,647.88	-------	NIL
Barclays Masterloan	19.9%	36	£108.89	£3,920.04	£272.16	NIL
Marks & Spencer	16.9%	36	£105.05	£3,781.80	£133.92	2 months interest
Abbey National	15.5%	36	£103.26	£3,717.36	£69.48	2 months interest

Based on a £3,000 loan over 3 years - source Money Facts.
Interest Rates correct at 29th July 1996

Hey, that's not bad!

What's more there are no hidden charges or administration fees.

How do I protect my payments?

You can arrange for our payment protection insurance, Scotgard, which secures your repayments in the event of illness, injury or unemployment. What's more, the premium is spread throughout the term of the loan, giving you repayment cover for just a small amount per month.

Terrific! What's that number again?

Freephone 0800 805 805. We are waiting for your call.

Yours sincerely

David Metcalfe

David Metcalfe
Personal Lending Manager

P.S. - Even better news for car buyers (or motorcycle, boats or caravans, for that matter!) Call us on **0800 805 805** and ask for full details of our brand new **50/50 Flexible Loan.** With APRs from just **13.9%***, this is designed specifically to give you lower repayments on higher value loans, to help you buy the car you really want.

* The 50/50 Flexible Loan allows you to reduce repayments by deferring repayments on part of the capital sum borrowed. A lump sum will be payable at the end of the loan term.

To apply for a loan you must be aged 18 or over. Full details and a written Consumer Credit quotation are available on request from Bank of Scotland, Teviot House, 41 South Gyle Crescent, Edinburgh EH12 9DR.

Telephone calls may be recorded for security purposes and may be monitored under the Bank's quality control procedures.

Bank of Scotland and   are the registered Trade Marks of the Governor and Company of the Bank of Scotland

Commentary

This advert uses the idea of turn-taking in spoken interactions to construct a fictional conversation between narrator and narratee. The narratee's responses are provided in italics, making sure that the reader can distinguish the two 'voices'.

In previous activities, it was noticed that real dialogue can range over many topics. In setting the advertising copy as a piece of dialogue, it seems as if the argument arrives at its endpoint through a natural progression, but of course the sequence is very tightly constructed: to test out the difference between this text and the real dialogue on p. 40 in terms of topic control, try blanking out the turns in italics in the advert, and get some informants to supply what they think might occur in the gaps. You will find that they are able to make some good guesses. They would not be able to predict the turns in the real conversation to such an extent.

During the interaction, the narratee is depicted as no push-over, but rather as a challenging customer, and in winning over this difficult narratee, the case of the company appears so much the more convincing. Winning over the narratee involves positioning him or her by means of some interesting presuppositions: for example, the initial question, which presupposes 'we wrote you a letter'; the narrator's third turn, which presupposes that the narratee has been thinking about home improvements and holidays. These presuppositions help construct the narratee as a sharp thinker whose main problem is lack of time – but busy, presumably, as a result of important work and not through unemployment. Helpfully, the narrator is able to provide all the relevant facts and figures which the narratee would have had to spend even more of his or her valuable time researching in order to arrive at the idea that Banking Direct is offering a very good deal.

The second page of this advert moves away from the spoken interaction format temporarily to include a very writerly piece of text in the form of a table. After this, the previous turn-taking continues: it seems that the narrator just broke off temporarily to wave a chart in front of the narratee, who is appropriately impressed. This is signalled by the use of 'Hey', expressing unexpected surprise, and the question 'How do I protect my payments?', which implies that the narratee is already thinking of making some. The final endorsement arrives in the form of the narratee asking for the company's phone number. The personal nature of the letter is then marked by the farewell greeting and signature, mirroring the use of the personal name of the addressee at the start.

57

But adverts don't have to set out their text in dialogue format in order to draw on spoken language.

Activity

How does Text: BP use the reader's knowledge of spoken language to convey its message? (In looking at the advert's strategies, don't forget to consider the aspects of language considered in Units 1–3 and in the earlier part of this unit.)

What is the advantage for the advertiser in using aspects of spoken language?

Commentary

The verbal language of this advertisement opens with the assumption that something has already happened: the reader has looked at the picture of the marine worms and exclaimed – 'shrieked'.

In a black and white format, some of the effect of the image is lost. In its original form, the worms are various shades of earth-brown, and have a very shiny lustre, reminding us of how wet they would be to the touch. They are coiled up on top of each other, caught by the camera in mid-motion, reminding us of their 'wriggly' behaviour; the image is in extreme close-up, so we are unable to avoid the idea of experiencing them, feeling them moving about on our skin. We can even see the fine details of their body parts. The advert, then, assumes that readers have displayed a kind of comic-strip reaction to these creepy-crawlies: 'ugh'! 'aargh'! 'yuk!' 'eek'!

This image is a good example of the kind of attention-seeking device mentioned in Unit 2, and the sentence in large type is another: the utterance is a bit of a puzzle until we relate it to the reaction we are supposed to have ourselves displayed. The text is putting us into the middle of a face-to-face, speech-like interaction, where part of the exchange has already taken place. As readers, we have already had our 'turn' in the turn-taking procedure characteristic of dialogue.

But, in order to make sense of all this, we need to be certain types of readers, and the first sentence of the copy (the body of the text after the 'hook' line in large type) tells us who we are: as narratees, we are 'most people' who 'recoil at the sight of a colony of marine worms'.

Even when we have worked out what the hook line is referring to, we still need to turn it into actual speech to make it work: certain words in the line need to be given more stress than others. So it is not until we

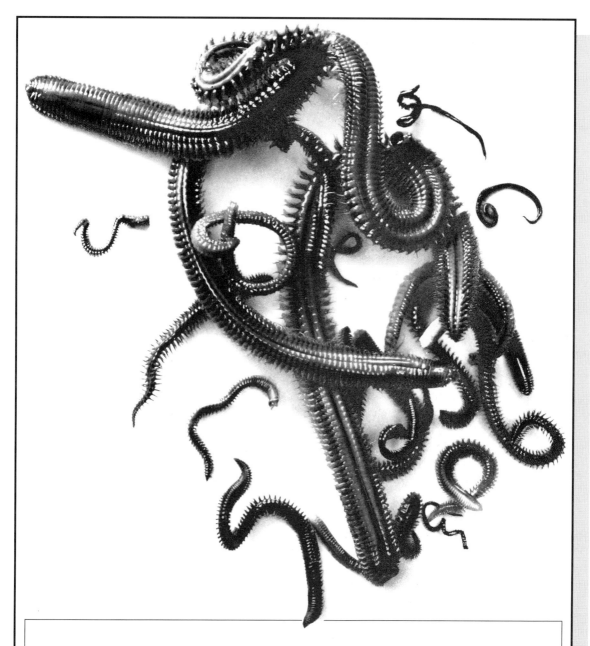

If one was missing we'd shriek.

Most people recoil at the sight of a colony of marine worms.

Here at BP we hold the 'lowest form of life' in somewhat higher regard.

Ever since our ecologists helped to unearth the fact that these friendless creatures are extremely sensitive. Particularly to any sudden chemical changes in sea water, their natural environment.

Apparently even minuscule quantities of pollutants can decimate entire worm colonies.

Of course we can't account for every single worm in the vicinity of our oil platforms.

But we can monitor their populations thereby detecting the first signs of contamination in time to prevent damage to the environment.

A prime example of the early bird catching the worm.

Protecting the environment is one of the things BP is doing today for all our tomorrows.

For all our tomorrows.

give the utterance some intonation that we can make it fit the rules of conversation: a turn must follow on from the one before, must be connected in some way. Given that we have already shrieked at what is in the picture, the line would have the following contrastive intonation:

If one was *missing, we'd* shriek.

This is the narrator telling us that at BP they would be upset and panicked to find they had lost any of their worms: BP's reaction would be opposite to ours.

In other ways, too, this text imitates spoken language. For a start, it teases us: it laughs at our reaction, punning on the words 'recoil' and 'unearth', and suggesting that we are rather mean to be horrified by the 'lowest form of life' who are 'these friendless creatures'. It uses a popular saying: 'the early bird catches the worm'. The lines are set out rather raggedly in order to get away from the idea that this is a written text of the 'textbook' type, and the expert voice disclaims his or her own expertise by using 'apparently' to pass on the wisdom of the marine ecologists. The narrator also uses links and structures more characteristic of speech than writing. For example, some of the utterances are either not full sentences, or only make complete sense when added to the previous element. Consider the need for the underlined items to refer to another element in order to make sense:

Ever since our ecologists helped to unearth the fact that these friendless creatures are extremely sensitive. *Particularly* to any sudden chemical changes in sea water, their natural environment.

The narrator also uses links which are characteristic of spoken language: for example, 'of course'.

The use of the word 'tomorrows' is interesting, too. In spoken language, we are much more tolerant of new coinages, in the form of either brand new words or adaptations of existing ones. The word 'tomorrow' is not normally used in the plural form. The whole phrase which contains it has two meanings: for all the tomorrows that will come one after another in future time; for the tomorrows that will be experienced by all of us. The use of 'our' here has shifted from the BP-owned sense of 'our ecologists' to the 'our' of the human race.

In framing this text in a speech-like, interactive way, the advertiser has constructed a close relationship between narrator and narratee which is more like a friendly exchange than a piece of communication from a large multinational company to an anonymous body of readers.

The advantages of this clever illusion hardly need spelling out.

One aspect of the narrator–narratee relationship could be considered further: is this text presuming a female narratee? Isn't it always women who are supposed to be frightened of creepy-crawlies? Would women, rather than men, be likely to be described as 'shrieking'? Might a female narratee account for the fact that the narrator plays down scientific discourse and plays up the idea of relationship? In surveys of public attitudes, is it not women, rather than men, who prioritise issues of the environment? Or is the narrator suggesting to us that, whatever our gender, we should adopt more of a supposedly female orientation towards science and technology – one which emphasises caring and community – and that this is what BP itself stands for?

We could find further evidence for these ideas by looking at where the text appeared: for example, we might have a different reading of this text in terms of the questions above if it appeared in *Marie Claire*, compared with *Loaded*. (Information about where the BP advert actually appeared is not available.)

'REALITY'

We looked previously at a piece of written discourse which was set out specifically in dialogue format, giving narrator and narratee 'parts' within a script; the BP text studied above was constructed in a way which presented a spoken interaction already happening. In both these cases, reference to the rules and conventions of the speech situation enabled the texts to draw the reader in and make him or her closely engaged in the action as it unfolds, in very much the same way as we participate in real face-to-face interactions.

But there is a further reason for texts to appear to open in mid-action, for them to jump right into the middle of things: this is to give them a sense of added reality, and to lessen our awareness of their constructed nature. In opening in the middle of the action, the text makes it appear as though we are chance observers of something that was going on before we came along, so the text acquires an independent existence and the status of 'reality'. This technique is a longstanding one in literary prose and film fiction: the text opens in the middle of a story, then we are given flashbacks that enable us to 'catch up'. The narrative power of this kind of construction is in the need the reader or audience will feel to be informed - this then justifies the flashback.

Activity

Text: ICI captures a scene in mid-action, then makes the narratee provide the flashback. Explain how this works – what does the narratee have to do, in order to understand this text?

(Note: there is no commentary on this advert.)

STEREOTYPING

Another aspect of spoken language which advertisers can exploit is how language varies across social groups. This idea was mentioned previously, but briefly, when it was suggested that the BP advert was perhaps trying to give a female orientation to the text.

Linguistics has gathered a large body of research on the social variation of language: that is, how factors such as age, gender, social class, ethnicity and region might affect language use. Since advertising tends to target particular groups of people, one way of getting an audience to recognise who an advert might be aimed at is to provide some language in the text that will be connected with a particular group. This connection doesn't have to be real in being language that is actually used by that group; it is enough that readers think there is some connection – a loose association is all that is required for advertising purposes. It is at this point that the process of **stereotyping** is clearly at work.

Social scientists would describe the process of stereotyping as one of the strategies human beings have for filtering all the information that is around us. Put simply, there is too much data in our environment for us to be able to deal with it in any detailed way. Our response is to process this data by singling out some of the details that we consider salient, or noteworthy, and using these to form categories that will help us fit our experiences into patterns that we can understand. So, for example, if someone invites us to a party, we already have a set of preformed expectations of what that will mean. The characteristics of 'partiness' for adults are likely to include music, chatting (and chatting up), dressing up, food (maybe), alcohol (for some groups, not all), a sense of celebration, and so on. If we embarked on every event and interaction with a blank mind and no expectations, then life would be very hard work. We would operate as adults in a childlike way, since children are, by the nature of their position, trying to form the categories that we take for granted in our adult lives.

Viewed in this way, stereotyping is a positive coping strategy. But its negative side is that categories are crude structures that can lead to us

Fortunately, over 300 million patients were able to count on our anaesthetics instead.

 World Class

closing our minds to the subtle complexities that really exist. Although stereotypes may have some connection with the idea or people they represent, they do not allow for individual variations – they are generalised, blanket descriptions; they often result in negative depictions, since they are commonly used by more powerful groups on less powerful ones; and they can lead to the stereotype-holders actually ignoring data that doesn't fit into their preconceived structures. To this extent, you could see stereotyping as a handy way for people to justify maintaining their own positions by not allowing those positions to be challenged.

Language often has an important role within the stereotyping process, as it is a quick way for us to generate a whole set of ideas about who people are and what they are like. One area where this can be seen clearly is in accent variation, and here TV adverts have used our stereotypes to powerful effect: the cheeky Cockney market traders who sing the praises of their wares; the Yorkshire-accented, stolid voice that stands for tradition and wholesomeness; the smooth RP (Received Pronunciation) accent that tells us about business and financial management. And advertisers can make new texts that show us, as a deliberate strategy, our own stereotypes: the glamorous woman who turns out to have a Lancashire accent and be called Gladys Allthorpe; the Asian family who speak to us in broad Glaswegian or Brummie tones.

Although written texts have only limited opportunity to conjure up accent (some do try to do this by alterations of spelling), written language can still suggest the nature of the speakers and therefore construct stereotypes both of the people being represented in the text and the people being addressed by it. This is not carried by the verbal text alone: the situation of the people featured, and the various aspects of language we termed 'paralanguage' earlier in this unit, will also play their part. Also, many written adverts exist as still-life versions of their TV counterparts, and the copywriters of written adverts can therefore assume that readers will bring their knowledge of the TV version with them when they read the written one.

Activity

Read Text: Castlemaine XXXX.

◎   Are there aspects of this text that you associate with 'maleness' in general?
◎   What does this advert suggest about the nature of Australian men?
◎   Do you think the text presupposes that the narratee is a particular gender?

Commentary

The subject of sport is one which is often associated with men. Cricket, in particular, connotes a picture of male players and a predominantly male crowd drinking cans of lager while watching the test match. There are terms in the speech bubble which require knowledge of cricket, without which the message is lost – the message being that in this particular game, many English (pommie) wickets have fallen, thus allowing plenty of the sponsor's cans to be sunk in celebration in the Australian bar in the picture. The idea of the relentless consumption of cans in itself presupposes knowledge of a male drinking ritual – every minor part of a sporting event can be an excuse to down another beer, accompanied by some form of spoken acknowledgement. At the centre of the text is the basic idea that sport often features as the primary content of male discourse.

There are further suggestions of maleness in the way the men are positioned at the bar – propped up adjacent to each other, drinking together and yet not being together, not really interacting at all. The slogan at the bottom of the page, 'wouldn't give a XXXX' can also be associated with maleness, in the stereotype of male speakers using swear words more freely than females – the idea that swearing is manly and positively 'unladylike'. The slogan suggests a kind of bad behaviour linguistically, and also indicates that, for Australian males at least, a particular kind of lager and a particular kind of sporting victory are top in their list of priorities in life.

The Australian male is depicted as a country hick, drinking in a ramshackle wooden bar in the middle of the outback, doggedly philistine. Male pride and identity are associated with their national team's unassailable cricketing performance. This is so routine that there is no surprise and therefore no emotion involved, hence the comatose expressions on the men's faces.

Some details give us clues that the text is very knowing about the way it is presenting itself and stereotyping the Australian male as a figure from the past: for example, the classic bush hats; the comic-strip speech bubble; the archaism of the phrase 'tests prove . . .', as well as the **pun** on the word 'tests' itself; and the way the text has its own rather old-fashioned looking picture frame, mirroring the pictures on the wall of the ancient bar and suggesting deliberate antiquity. Modern adverts often adopt an ironic stance of this kind, suggesting that they don't take themselves too seriously, so the audience shouldn't. This is another strategy, of course, for getting traditional stereotypes past the reader, whose protests can then be dismissed as a humourless reaction to an obvious joke.

The advert makes strong associations between maleness and cricket, maleness and lager drinking, and Australian maleness and both. Although the narratee is constructed as male, women readers take a range of meanings from the text, too. These meanings tell them generally about the supposed nature of men and, more specifically, about the supposed nature of Australian men.

Extension

This unit has covered many aspects of spoken language, in an attempt to consider how written adverts can use aspects of speech to create certain effects. Below are some suggestions for taking these ideas further.

Collect some written adverts that refer to speech or use aspects of spoken interaction. For example, adverts that:

◎   represent prosodic features, such as intonation and stress
◎   represent turn-taking or other specific markers of interaction
◎   use ellipsis and presupposition
◎   pitch the reader into the middle of a 'story' where events have already taken place
◎   suggest that members of social groups use language in a particular way, including what they talk about as well as how they express themselves.

In analysing the texts you have collected, consider any relevant aspects from Units 1–3, particularly the role of images, layouts and typographical features, and the relationship between narrator and narratee.

Nautical but nice: intertextuality

The term **intertextuality** refers to the way one text can point to or base itself on another. For example, the phrase in the unit title, 'nautical but nice', is a piece of intertextuality, in that it is a variation of an older slogan 'naughty but nice', originally used to describe cream cakes (and reputedly invented by Salman Rushdie). The phrase 'nautical but nice' was used during 1995 to describe a car which was advertised by being pictured on a cliff-top, pointing out to sea.

Intertextuality can be an important component of an advert's meaning, in that the original text being referred to established a message which the second text can then use and elaborate on. In this way, the second text doesn't have to work so hard – it can take for granted that the original text has left a trace which it can use to its advantage. In the above example, the 'naughty but nice' slogan suggested the sensual, forbidden delight of eating cream cakes. For those people who remember the original advert, the memory or 'trace' will involve this idea, and although the car wasn't being sold as an edible commodity, it does no harm for readers to associate cars with forbidden pleasure.

For intertextuality to work completely, readers have to be able to remember the original advert and place the reference being established. But if they don't, it doesn't matter too much, for the contemporary advert will simply be enigmatic, and this in itself is useful: people will be forced to ask others what it's going on about. Keeping themselves talked about is the main aim of adverts; the worst fate for them is to be ignored.

Advertising is a relatively young form of discourse compared with, say, literature. And yet it is now old enough to have a history in the same way that literature has. So, just as modern literary writers can base their stories on traditional texts, modern advertising copywriters can base their copy on older versions. The effect of this strategy in either type of discourse can be the same: we feel clever if we 'get' the connection. The difference is that not everyone may recognise a reworking of a Shakespearian plot, but many people are likely to remember an advertising slogan or jingle - they seem to stick in the mind, sometimes for irritatingly long periods of time.

Activity

To explore ideas about the shelf-life of advertising language, read through the list of old and contemporary slogans and jingles in Text: Slogans. First, see if you can add to the list. Then investigate the question of who recognises them: for example, do people of different ages have stores of different slogans?

Text: Slogans

The Esso sign means happy motoring,
The Esso sign means happy motoring,
The Esso sign means happy motoring,
Call at the Esso sign.

A million housewives every day
Pick up a can of beans and say
Beanz Meanz Heinz.

Vorsprung Durch Technik.

The bank that likes to say 'Yes'.

The lion goes from strength to strength.

The Listening Bank.

Who would you like to have a One-to-One with?

We won't make a drama out of a crisis.

Which twin has the Toni?

Boom boom boom boom, Esso Blue.

Shake and vac and put the freshness back.

A Mars a day helps you work, rest and play.

All around the house spring clean with Flash.

Domestos kills all known germs.

The crumbliest, flakiest chocolate - tastes like chocolate never tasted before.

All because the lady loves Milk Tray.

Have a break - have a Kit-Kat.

Snap, crackle and pop.

Just do it.

Coke is it.

Commentary

Although many of these are from TV texts, there is a close relationship between moving adverts and written ones – in itself a form of inter-textuality. This means that when we see a written slogan, we can often supply the soundtrack. For example, when you read the Castlemaine XXXX advert in the previous unit, you might have 'heard' the buzzing of flies, the sound of a didgeridoo, an Australian male voice announcing that 'Australians wouldn't give a XXXX for anything else'. You might also have supplied an appropriate voice for the speech in the bubble.

The slogans you have been exploring come from different eras, from the 1950s to the present day. People of different ages will recognise some, but not others. Rather than this being a problem, advertisers can use these differences to their advantage. For example, if a company wants to target older people, playing on a slogan they will recognise from their youth will have at least two positive effects: it will create a sense of nostalgia in the target audience; and it will make them feel 'special' in that a code is being used that they recognise, but others don't – a similar effect as that created by the use of German in the BA advert in Unit 3.

Younger groups can also be targeted by means of reference to older slogans and catch-phrases. Often this is about rebellion, acted out ling-uistically – turning the older generations' nice sentiments into in-your-face statements. For example, the initialism TGIF (thank God it's Friday), adapted by Crunchie adverts some years ago ('Thank Crunchie it's Friday') has a new version, in the form of the title of a TV programme aimed at a youth audience: TFI Friday. Like the Castlemaine XXXX advert, the producers manage to break taboo ('Thank fuck it's Friday') without having to come right out with it and, as a result, be accused of offensiveness. Also, since the swear words are represented only by initials, the producers could always pretend innocence ('Thank fudge it's Friday'?). Slogans which secretly encode taboo words are often aimed at a young audience: they can satisfy a desire to sneak forbidden artefacts past one's parents, smuggled into the respectable living-room right under their noses.

Intertextuality is no observer of boundaries: it doesn't have to involve a particular slogan for a specific product. It can move between advertising and many other forms of discourse: for example, popular sayings with no author (who invented TGIF in the first place?); traditional literary texts with well-known authors; film texts and film styles (such as the Boddington's parody of the Hollywood musical folly); even TV station logos, with their signature music (such as the Channel 4 logo which breaks up into a happy face, smoking a Hamlet cigar). And advertising can, of course, play with whole styles of earlier advert: for example, the Castlemaine XXXX advert refers deliberately to an older genre of advertising when it uses the phrase 'Tests prove . . .', a genre where a scientific expert reported on supposedly objective findings from experiments. We now consider such adverts to be rather tacky, and so reference to them can establish an in-joke shared by narrator and narratee.

Intertextuality can also occur between texts from the same era, with one product or service using another's established name or slogan to enhance its own publicity. For example, Farley's Junior Milk advertised itself by picturing one baby watching another perform feats of amazing strength and agility. The slogan was 'I'll bet he drinks Farley's Junior Milk', in imitation of the Carling Black Label advert. In this case, the milk product is benefiting from the connotations of remarkable power associated with Carling Black Label. But intertextuality can also be contrastive, pointing out differences rather than similarities. For example, here is the slogan from a current NSPCA advert, written below the picture of a puppy and above the seasonally occurring line 'A dog is for life, not just for Christmas':

Toys Aren't Us

Activity

Text: *Time* magazine is an advert using intertextual reference to an earlier advert. Do you know the original advert being referred to? If so, explain how the intertextuality works. If not, what reading do you have of this advert – what sense can you make of it?

Commentary

This text is referring to an earlier advert featuring the same 'pregnant' man. The older advert was produced in the 1970s for the British Pregnancy Advisory Service, and its aim was to make men more aware of contraception and to get them to take more responsibility for it. The original slogan read 'Would you be more careful if it were you that got pregnant?'

The paralanguage of the text is very noticeable: the man's doleful expression and his very unfashionable haircut and clothes (unfashionable even in the 1970s) suggest innocence and possible abandonment. He is unhappy to be pregnant, he has been a victim of his own trusting nature. He is poor and lonely.

When the advert came out, it caused a storm, readers complaining that it was unpleasant, tasteless and freakish. As with the Gossard and 18–30 Holiday adverts discussed in Unit 2, this furore shot the advert to instant fame. It is probably obvious even now, two decades later, why audiences found the text so disturbing. After all, we still live with the idea that even 'natural' (i.e. female) pregnancy should be hidden away in shame. For example, in 1988 the singer Neneh Cherry provoked a strong public reaction when she appeared on 'Top of the Pops' and performed while several months pregnant. The locus of complaint seemed to relate to the fact that not only was she very pregnant, but she had made no attempt to hide it – she performed in a short lycra, figure-hugging skirt. She was refusing to be ashamed of herself.

The pregnant man, then, probably raised a whole host of cultural taboos: not only in making the idea of pregnancy very visible, but by presenting a man in a female 'condition'. Aside from the pregnant state, he is also smooth-skinned, slight of frame, and exhibiting almost a parody of the helpless abandoned doe-eyed female. The very blokish clothes tell us he is a man; but his body language is all female. These contradictory messages are intended to disturb and are likely to do so, especially when they are uttered in a culture where it is much more acceptable for women to aspire to male characteristics than vice versa.

Another area of cultural difficulty is that advances in medical science are forcing us constantly to confront ethical issues: for example, at the time of writing, a woman in her fifties has just given birth to a child whose genetic parents are the woman's own daughter and son-in-law. Debate has revolved round the relationships and connections here, such as whether the child is the older woman's daughter or granddaughter. The modern advert refers to the idea of medical science in its use of the word 'insertion', which suggests that the man's pregnancy could be the

Text: *Time* magazine

It only took one insertion to make this man world famous.

Advertising is news when it's in TIME magazine. After just one appearance in a TIME editorial feature, this man was a celebrity.

Thanks to the fact that more people worldwide turn to our pages for their news than to any other single source.

So if you want advertising that gets noticed, you know what to do. Make sure all your insertions are in the right place.

TIME
Our cover sells.

result of a biological breakthrough; the term also functions as a mock euphemism for sexual penetration. It is only when we read the small print at the bottom that we realise the advert is selling advertising space in *Time* magazine, and 'insertion' also means putting an advert into a space. Our narrator has caught us out – our dirty minds sprang to all the wrong conclusions. However, the final line of the text brings us back to ideas of sex again by jokingly issuing a warning to its narratees: 'make sure all your insertions are in the right place'. The narrator is presuming his narratees are male: it is men who insert. Or perhaps the suggestion is that narratees of either sex need to adopt stereotypically male behaviour – getting noticed, being assertive, forthright and thrusting. If they do this, using *Time*'s advertising space, they can succeed in terms of the enterprise culture: world fame after one appearance.

Activity

Text: NSPCC (2) is an advert from the 1996 campaign. The advert does not make reference to another single advert, as the one from *Time* magazine did; but it is still operating a kind of intertextuality.

What observations can you make about the way this text works? You may wish to compare it with the NSPCC text you studied in Unit 2. In analysing the advert below, don't forget to consider all the textual features that have been covered in Units 1–4.

(Note: there is no commentary on this activity.)

Extension

This unit has covered a range of different ways in which adverts can use intertextuality. Here are some ideas for taking these aspects further:

1   Collect some adverts that refer to or imitate non-advertising texts. For example, adverts that look like newspaper articles, poems, instruction manuals, letters, etc. Analyse how they work; also consider what adverts gain by referring to texts that are outside their own 'system'.
2   Collect some TV and written adverts for the same product. Assess how far the written text assumes knowledge of the spoken TV one.
3   Collect some adverts that refer back in time to an advert or advertising style of the past. Ask a group of people of different ages to respond to the texts, to see if they 'get' the references. When

My father never laid a finger on me. Bastard.

This is David's story.

'My brother was always my dad's favourite. But he just ignored me.

I really tried hard to impress him but it never seemed to be enough.

When I got 96% in a maths exam I thought I might get a 'well done'. Instead he asked me what happened to the other 4%. He loves sport, but he never once came to watch me playing in the school team.

I didn't know what I had to do to get him to like me, let alone love me.

The worst thing is, his attitude to me affected the way I was treating my own children. My wife could see it was destroying us as a family and suggested I got help. I'm now having counselling which is helping me deal with the way I'd been made to feel.'

As David's story shows, child abuse isn't just about sexual assault and physical brutality. Emotional cruelty may be less obvious, but the effects can be just as devastating.

Imagine always being criticized, shouted at or even totally ignored.

They can all lead to feelings of low self-worth and depression.

And, as in David's case, the anger created is sometimes transferred to the victim's own children.

Because of all this, the NSPCC is launching 'A Cry for Children'. It's a cry to everyone to stop and think about the way they behave towards children. To recognise the impact that any form of cruelty can have on a child. And to realise the way children are treated affects their whole lives.

Please answer the cry.

If you, or someone you know is suffering abuse, please call the NSPCC Child Protection Helpline on 0800 800 500. Or if, after reading this, you'd find more information helpful, please call us on 0171 825 2775.

NSPCC
A cry for children.

you look at your results, think about the products that are using historical references and the age group they might be targeting.

4   Survey some adverts aimed at young people. Are there particular styles adopted which symbolise rebellion and a rejection of the previous generation's ideas?

5   Collect some adverts that refer to other contemporary adverts.

Consider what the advantage might be for the adverts in question to refer to others.

Cultural variations

The previous unit highlighted the way in which advertising texts can sometimes refer to or base themselves on other texts of all kinds. For readers to understand the references that are being made, they have to have some knowledge of the textual systems in their culture – that is, what types of text are in existence and the way texts of all kinds work. This knowledge is cultural knowledge, in that different cultures may well have different categories of texts and different rules about how they operate. For example, one basic rule about texts in English-speaking cultures is that they operate from left to right: this is the way English writing is read, and this is the way you are making sense of my writing at this moment. This rule is at the base of many 'before and after' sequences, such as those in washing powder adverts where the soiled garment on the left becomes the pristine article on the right. This sequence can be 'read' so clearly by us that words of explanation are not really needed: the brand name is all that is required for us to attribute the miraculous change to the agency of the product. This textual ordering is so much taken for granted in the West that when a large soap powder manufacturer advertised in the Middle East it was assumed that no changes were needed to the advert, apart from a verbal translation. But Arabic readers read from right to left, as this is the way Arabic script operates. So for audiences in the Middle East, the product was offering to turn their clothes from snowy white to grimy grey. Needless to say, sales of this particular powder were rather disappointing (Cook 1992).

As well as having different structural rules about how texts work, different cultures bring different attitudes and values to the reading of any text. If advertisers do not take account of these differences, or if they try to break them down, they need to expect difficulty, if not outright failure. One example of failure for this reason was Volvo's attempt in 1990 to market a car in the same way across the whole of Europe. The campaign was soon dropped through lack of response, and Volvo went back to some previously accepted traditions - promoting the car's safety to Swiss and UK audiences; its status to French audiences; for Swedish audiences, its economy; and for Germans, its performance (Brierley 1995).

Perhaps the clearest way that cultural variations can be demonstrated is in the area of verbal translation. Translators know that the essence of good advertising copy is not about simply translating the words; it is about encoding the right concepts, and those concepts may well vary from culture to culture - as in the car examples, above. This process is called **copy adaptation** - adapting the text to fit the culture of its targeted group.

BRAND NAMES

Despite the attention paid within advertising agencies to the whole business of targeting specific groups, there have been some spectacular failures to get it right when companies have tried to go international or global with their products. This has been for a variety of reasons. Sometimes, the brand name of the product has unfortunate associations when translated into other languages. Looking at this area can illustrate how powerful the operation of connotation is - the way in which words can call up associations in our minds. Because of the way we make connections between words and particular ideas, feelings and experiences, brand names are crucial for advertisers. They are very economic, acting as little concentrated capsules of meaning. Where advertisers get it right, readers will do the work to generate all the intended connotations.

There are whole companies who specialise in offering research on brand-name connotations to product manufacturers looking for a name for a new product, or looking at how best to market an existing product to new, foreign audiences. These companies - for example Interbrand, and The Brandnaming Company - typically organise brainstorming sessions where they ask groups of people to let their imaginations 'roam free', from which meetings they arrive at shortlists of names whose suitability is then researched further. Names on the shortlist have to pass certain tests: for example, that they are not too close to existing names; that they are pronounceable in all the world's major languages; that they have the right connotations. The latter, however, is a complex area. Even within one language, connotations can be about quite subtle distinctions. For example, when Pickfords Travel merged with Hogg Robinson two years ago, the shortlist for the new company name had two main contenders: 'Destinations', and 'Going Places'. The new company chose the latter, deciding that 'destinations' tended to suggest long-haul flights to far-flung places – travel for the privileged. 'Going Places', on the other hand, was thought to describe all sorts of travel and therefore be more suitable for the mass market, which was the company's target. Interestingly, the phrase 'going places' also suggests aspiration – we talk about ambitious career people 'going places', while there is something of the meaning of foregone conclusion about 'destinations', an idea of destiny as something fixed and unalterable, and a destination as a fixed point to which we are directed. The mass market is much more likely to identify with the idea of moving up and on, while affluent audiences are arguably going to be more comfortable about the idea of fixedness, since this underpins the idea of inheritance, the opposite of 'self-made'. In the word 'going', there is also the sense of continuous activity in the grammatical 'ing' form, and a suggestion of success, as in the phrase 'a going concern', which attaches to the company as well as to its customers. The French/Latin origin of 'destinations', compared with the Anglo-Saxon 'going places', also connotes elite versus democratic, and abstract versus concrete to English-speaking audiences.

The fact that producers are willing to pay significant amounts of money to brand-name consultants is an indication of the extent to which success or failure is thought to rest with this aspect of advertising language: for example, a shortlist of three names to cover just the UK market typically costs £15,000; a corporate name for use world wide is likely to cost more in the region of £90,000.

Given that connotations within a single language can involve some complex aspects of meaning, as above, it's not surprising that marketing departments are prepared to pay up; and the advertising industry has its fair share of translation disasters, as a salutary lesson to those who might be tempted to go it alone in a foreign market.

Car companies appear to be particularly accident-prone. While some are spotted in time – for example, Rolls Royce realised that its Silver Mist would not be received well in Germany, as 'mist' means excrement – others are launched before the error is revealed. Two examples of the latter include Nissan's 'Pantry Boy' and Ford's 'Pinto'; to its Brazilian customers, 'pinto' translated as a slang word for 'tiny male genitals'. Slang is rarely encoded in dictionaries; nor are connotations in general, as dictionary definitions tend to base themselves on **denotation** – a word's

Susannah Hart, Interbrand Director, displays some brand names that fail the connotation test for English speaking audiences.

barest, referential meaning. For example, in a standard English dictionary, the denotative meaning of the terms 'bachelor' and 'spinster' are 'unmarried adult male' and 'unmarried adult female', respectively. But these terms have strong connotations, traditionally positive in the case of bachelor and negative in the case of spinster. But even this isn't the end of the story. Some younger speakers of English, particularly women, might have more positive connotations for the word 'spinster' than tradition suggests, as there has been some attempt to change the profile of this word and 'reclaim' it. In the end, connotations are learnt through daily discourse with speakers, not through dictionaries.

The same is true of **metaphorical** meaning, a non-literal level of meaning where one thing is represented as another. Here, dictionaries can be positively misleading, often encoding the literal meaning but leaving out the metaphorical one. Someone trying to make sense of **idiomatic language** in general - expressions where the overall meaning cannot be derived from the sum of the parts - faces the same problem. Where there is no awareness that an expression is metaphorical or idiomatic, a translator may give a literal version and, in so doing, create a completely different meaning. This occurred when the Pepsi slogan, 'Come alive with the Pepsi generation' was translated into Chinese as 'Pepsi will bring your ancestors back from the dead'; Kentucky Fried Chicken's 'finger lickin' good' did little better in Chinese as 'eat your finger off'.

Polysemy (one word having more than one meaning) is often exploited consciously in advertising: one example of this is the **pun** on the word 'insertion' in the *Time* magazine advert in Unit 5. But in translation, alternative meanings may be called up unwittingly. This was the case when the Parker Pen company marketed a ballpoint pen in Mexico. The copy was supposed to read 'It won't leak in your pocket and embarrass you'. But the word for embarrass in Spanish, 'embarazar', can mean something else, too. For the Spanish-speaking audience, an alternative reading of the final copy was:

It won't leak in your pocket and make you pregnant.

Unintentional polysemy can also occur within language. For example, the mobile phone operator, Orange, is about to develop its product in Northern Ireland. As a result, it is having to rethink its existing slogan, which has an unintentionally political meaning when applied to that area:

The future's bright, the future's Orange.

The phonology, or sound system, of a language also plays its part in the creation of meaning - in, for example, **sound symbolism**, where we associate sounds with particular ideas. In a short expression such as a brand name, individual sounds are thrown into relief and must therefore be chosen with care.

You can see the operation of sound symbolism in the way certain sounds often occur in the brand names of particular types of product: for example, fricative sounds such as 'f', 'v', and 'sh' are often present in the names of household cleaners in English, such as 'Flash', 'Frish', and the older 'Vim'. The suggestion is efficacy through the possession of abrasive qualities. These sounds are unlikely to occur in the names of emollient facial creams or moisturisers (although when these are marketed to men rather than women, it is often a different story). Although such associations are strongly felt by the users of a particular language, they are culture specific and often do not translate.

Other aspects of phonology are also relevant. For example, sequences of syllables in one language may be whole words in another. This was the case for 'Coca Cola', which in Chinese means 'bite the wax tadpole'; the Vauxhall Nova bemused its Spanish audience, for whom 'no va' means 'won't go'; Toyota's MR2, said aloud by French speakers, sounds very similar to *merde*, French for 'shit'.

Product brand names and slogans, like the advertising copy itself, are also subject to the processes of language change. These processes themselves are not simply linguistic: language change reflects changes in the world around us, both in terms of physical realities and in terms of attitudes and values. One area of language that is relatively unstable is that of **euphemism**: the coinage of 'polite' language that enables us not to have to confront aspects of life we find difficult or embarrassing, such as sex, death and bodily functions. Euphemistic terms rapidly degenerate and, as they do so, new euphemisms have to be coined to take their place and save our blushes. For example, look at Text: Lavvo, from a 1937 edition of *Woman and Home*. At that time, the term 'lavatory' was a euphemism, taken from a Latin root, 'lavabo', meaning 'to wash'. (The more modern term, 'toilet', is a euphemism from the French word *toile*, meaning 'a washing cloth'.) Nowadays, a product called 'Lavvo' would seem rather comically direct.

Text: Lavvo

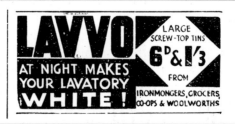

Taboo – the idea of some areas as 'forbidden' and therefore unable to be mentioned – can apply to social groups as well as particular experiences. For example, in the 1970s, sales of Guinness had fallen as a result of younger drinkers moving to lager, and Guinness launched a new campaign for the 1980s, designed to target the people who drank Guinness only occasionally, with the intention of getting them to become more regular consumers. Their campaign was a humorous parody of a charity or phobia group, with the slogan 'Friends of the Guinnless'. Although initially sales rose considerably, soon the joke wore thin and the slogan was seen in a negative light.

When their campaign failed, the company turned away from social realism towards surrealism, featuring Rutger Hauer as a sage-like figure in enigmatic and mysterious landscapes. The new slogan, 'Pure Genius', reversed the previous idea of something lacking (Brierley 1995).

It can be very revealing of cultural changes to look at the way one type of product has been advertised over a number of years, particularly if that product touches on an area of cultural taboo.

Activity

Text: Tampax is an advert from a 1996 campaign featuring in magazines aimed at young girls (for example *Sugar*, *Bliss*, *Enjoy*). Following it, in Text: Older adverts are some adverts that featured in women's magazines in the 1930s and 1950s.

◎ What language differences do you observe in the adverts from these different eras?

◎ What do you surmise about some of the cultural changes that have occurred over the years, in attitudes towards menstruation?

Commentary

Compared with the older texts, the modern one is extremely explicit, resembling in its content more a set of instructions for use than the few well-chosen words we've come to think of as characteristic of advertising language. There are elements of intertextuality here: as well as being a set of instructions, the text could also be, at first glance, a newspaper article or a problem page. The idea of an information text is suggested visually by the typographical features of column layout and darker print at the top of each column. These intertextual references are not accidental, of course: instructions, news articles and problem pages all share the idea of

When you were around a year old, you were such a determined little thing.

No staircase went unscaled. No cupboard went unexplored.

And when you decided you wanted to walk, you weren't about to let the odd bump on your bum put you off.

So what makes you so faint-hearted now you're older?

The fact is that everyone, yes everyone, takes a few goes to get the hang of inserting a tampon. (That's why we're giving you some free samples to experiment with.)

And those exact same people who all struggled at first are now using them without giving it a second thought.

Of course, like walking, it's a whole lot easier if you've got someone to lend a helping hand and offer advice. So here goes:

Firstly, what exactly happens when you start trying to use a tampon?

It may well feel as if there is no proper opening for it.

Rest assured, all girls are built the same.

Patience, time and relaxation will allow you to find the right place. And the same qualities will allow you to gently insert it.

Tampax tampons come in mini sizes so it will never feel as though you are stretching yourself uncomfortably.

It's also a good idea to test out how the applicator works outside your body before you use it.

Then, when you fully understand the mechanics, throw that one away and use a fresh one. (Another good reason for those free samples we're giving you.)

The trick is to aim the tampon at the small of your back, rather than straight up. You'll find the applicator will leave the tampon in exactly the right place.

And don't worry, it is physically impossible for a tampon to get lost inside you and equally impossible for it to drop out.

Right, now you have finally got it inside you, here's all the good news.

Tampax tampons expand lengthways and widthways, so there's no need to worry about leaking.

Just change it about every four to

eight hours. (Whenever you pull the cord and feel the tampon start to slide out easily.)

And by the way, the cord won't break because it's sewn into the fabric of the tampon.

Now you've got the hang of tampons, you may find you need never use towels again.

After all, you grew out of nappies rather a long time ago.

**the
last time
you
had trouble
getting
the
hang of
something,
you didn't
give up so
easily.**

GOOD NEWS *for* WOMEN

(Especially those who are married)

❦

IT'S plain common sense to be cautious about new ideas, until they're proved to be *good* as well as new. But once you know that thousands and thousands of women have tried out a new idea, and found it *better in every way*, it's sheer prejudice to cling to old-fashioned methods.

Undreamed of Comfort

TAKE Tampax, for example. This new, *completely different* form of monthly sanitary protection has brought undreamed of comfort to countless women, who hesitated at first about testing it. Designed by a doctor, with specialised knowledge of women's problems on 'those difficult days', Tampax is *worn internally*. It's daintier, safer, simpler. It's quite invisible and cannot cause odour, chafing or discomfort. Easily disposable, too.

A Personal Test

WHY not test Tampax yourself. Just send 6d. in stamps to The Nurse, Tampax Limited, Dept. 26A, Belvue Road, Northolt, Middlesex, asking for *either* Regular Tampax No. 1 (suitable for all normal needs) *or* Super Absorbent Tampax No. 2, which gives 40% more absorbency for those who need more than average protection. Samples will be sent under plain cover.

Now that you can easily obtain the finest of all at ordinary price, it is wise to ask by name for Camelia. So soft . . . so sure . . .

Camelia

towels with loops

TRY THIS NEW HEALTH PLAN FOR SIX MONTHS

Join the movement started by British women doctors, for the abolition of 'Woman's Handicap.'

Here's a relief and release for you ! . . . all of you who take it for granted that you must put up with a few days of misery every month . . . whose work is upset, social life restricted, freedom and happiness curtailed by discomforts and sufferings you think are inevitable. Follow the lead of British women doctors. Join this movement to rid you of a needless handicap. Send for the Health Plan samples that are offered below and learn all about it. A doctor explains the plan in a clear concise little book called 'Women of Today' which will be sent to you.

The plan is simplicity itself, consisting more of discarding old habits than of learning new ones—although a few new ones must be acquired. Thousands of the young women of to-day owe their splendid unfailing fitness to it, and their capacity to achieve success. Thousands more are even now achieving, by means of it, a complete transformation of their lives. 'To think of all the years I have been handicapped—apparently quite unnecessarily,' writes one of them. 'If "Women of To-day" had come my way six years instead of six months ago, believe me, my life up to date would have been a very different story.'

Write to-day for the Health Plan samples and, starting with the new year, follow the plan faithfully for a full six months. You will be grateful to it for life.

LILIA

THE BRITISH SOLUBLE SANITARY TOWEL
Standard size 1/- per carton of 12,
with loops (or without them).

SPECIAL HEALTH PLAN OFFER: The new Health Plan Booklet, 6 assorted Lilia towels, and a suspender belt, for 1/-; Booklet, 12 towels, one pair two-purpose directoire knickers in luxury Courtaulds suède locknit (colours: Ivory, Peach, Black), with removable protective shield, and a suspender belt for 5/- (S.W. and W. sizes; W.X. 1/- extra). All post free and in plain cover. Write: Miss D. Downing, Dept. N2, Sashena Ltd., Lilia Works, Bartholomew Road, London, N.W.5.

Awarded Certificate of the Institute of Hygiene.

Carus
SANITARY TOWELS

Regd

She's so natural

no one could help liking her. Her easy manner
and gay smile suggest she has never a care in the
world. On 'tiresome' days she finds confidence
in the extra absorbency and greater comfort
which Carus towels provide. And naturally she
appreciates the fact that they are made by Carus
of Darwen, who specialise in the manufacture of
surgical dressings.

MEXSOL disposable towels 1/9 doz.   Junior size 1/8 doz.
OMEX cotton wool towels in four sizes.   2/8½ to 4/1 doz.
Junior size, 2/3 doz.   All looped.

factual information-giving associated more with 'truth' than with persuasion. Two of the older texts – the Tampax and Lilia adverts – also adopt information formats. However, they share a tone of sobriety which is very different from the modern advert, which presents a narrator who is just as much of an expert as the narrators in the older texts, but who talks as a friend, in a style which owes much to spoken language.

The older texts preserve the idea of taboo in talking about menstruation, using euphemisms such as 'tiresome days' and, in the case of the Camelia text, just a calendar to signify the unmentionable subject. In the Tampax advert, it is particularly married women who are thought to be knowledgeable about you-know-what. Where menstruation is discussed, the discourse is medical and of physical illness: 'surgical dressings', 'women's handicap', 'new health plan', 'the Nurse'. Some mitigation is offered through the connotation of 'naturalness' in such items as flowers and puppies, but these only exist as vague symbols of femininity, not of menstruation itself.

The modern text is in rebellion against these unspoken cultural ideas. Not only are there explicit details of what you put where, and not only is there a humorous approach to an erstwhile deadly serious subject, but the appearance of the whole advert inverts accepted norms of presentation. For example, the hookline is at the bottom rather than the top; the cut-out coupon comes first, rather than last; the cartoon-style image is on the right rather than, as often happens, on the left. The notion of a 'problem' is still present; but this text suggests that the problem is to do with acquiring a new skill, rather than the problem being menstruation itself. The reference to nappies is very clever: internally worn tampons, for many years leaders in the market, have recently suffered a serious challenge from a new generation of externally worn sanitary towels – characterised as 'nappies' in the modern text. In the older Tampax advert, the established market was the sanitary towels, and it was Tampax that was the newcomer.

Comparing adverts through time, as here, can demonstrate how public attitudes to subjects have changed and how these changes are reflected in the language used. But before we get too smug about how far we have come in dealing with sensitive subjects, it would be useful to remember that *blue* liquid is still used in TV demonstrations of sanitary towels, through fear of being too explicit. (The modern Tampax advert you have been studying was originally blue, as well.)

Advertising is often an index of attitudes because, in order for an advert to work, it must tap into some thinking 'out there' in the marketplace. But it would be a mistake to think that adverts are a simple reflection of how we all are, in some natural way. Advertising, as a very public form of discourse, is also part of the way we construct our ideas about the world around us: what people are like, who does what, who is important and why, what we should be worried about, and so on. So advertising often taps into what it itself has helped to create. For example, who is it that needs to be protected from the idea of menstruation? In a 'natural' world, surely not women themselves. If women are embarrassed by it, then that is a result of the way they are made to feel. Part of the discourse of advertising is to problematise aspects of life that can then be 'solved' by means of a product.

Ideas we receive about the world through advertising are all driven by who the advertisers think is likely to do the purchasing (or make the decision to purchase), and what that group needs to think about itself in order to spend money on the product. If large amounts of disposable income were thought to reside with disabled people, lone parents, black groups, or lesbians, our adverts would tell us very different stories.

Activity

To consider the idea that advertising constructs a 'reality' for its narratees, read through Text: Wartime adverts. These are all from *Woman and Home*, 9 April 1944.

How do these texts set out a picture of expected behaviour for their female narratees?

Commentary

During World War II, women did many jobs previously considered male – such as welding, munitions assembly, and various types of work in the armed forces. But after the war, women were expected to go back into the home and give up these jobs to the returning men. For many women who had experienced being valued in paid employment, this was an extremely difficult transition to make. Comparing women's magazines in the early 1940s with their equivalent post-war publications is very revealing. While in the war years, particularly early on, magazines were full of women engaged in active and meaningful public work, the 1950s saw a plethora of complex cooking recipes, knitting and needlework patterns, and articles about the minutiae of domestic arrangements, with women again exclusively tending hearth and home.

The adverts you have been reading strike an interesting balance between exhorting women to make more patriotic war effort – growing more vegetables, keeping fit, being part of communal living – and reminding them of their proper sphere, which is to be in the private home and to appear 'feminine'. The Oatine advert projects an idea of the 'lovely girl' to aspire to when the war is over; the Day and Martin's text calls up the adage 'Keep the home fires burning'; the Ministry of Agriculture reminds readers of the original 'woman's place' by enlarging the word 'garden' and giving it a hyphen, contrasting it with the unspoken but expected word, 'home'; in the Crawford's advert, the woman longs for 'a fresh set of chair covers'; the Odo-Ro-No advert problematises the idea of shared living space by raising worries about personal hygiene. Did women in 1944 really equate their future happiness with cream crackers, and were women who were sleeping rough in the London Underground stations really fretting about their perspiration stains? Another type of text which often occurred alongside adverts such as these perhaps gives us better insights into real life, compared with the constructed reality of advertising discourse. This was the stern government warning, through information about sexually transmitted diseases, that women should remain monogamous and, as they put it, 'live cleanly'. The fact was that, despite the appalling suffering and privations that war entailed, women were temporarily out of the control of marriage and nuclear family structures, upon which much of commercial consumerism is based. It is often at points where the consumers might escape that advertising discourse is at its most strident.

In 1944, there were hopes of victory for the Allies, but it was not yet certain. The adverts combine the idea that women should still work for the war effort with the suggestion that they should prepare themselves to be concerned with less momentous events – like the availability of cream crackers.

Activity

This unit began with the idea of looking across different cultures, and it was suggested that different cultures bring different sets of attitudes and values to texts. It may also be true that different cultures vary in the extent to which certain ideas are taboo – an issue that was raised in Unit 5, in considering the *Time* magazine advert of the 'pregnant' man.

Text: IL Returpapper is a Swedish advert for recycling: the company funding the advert is called IL Returpapper, and the text appeared in a monthly magazine entitled *Manadsjournalen,* a glossy publication featuring a range of different articles and aimed at both sexes. It resembles the magazine supplements of British broadsheet newspapers in format,

Text: Wartime adverts

WAR-TIME REFLECTIONS

To be the lovely girl you mean to be when your war-time job is finished, take care of your complexion to-day. Do not be tempted to use unknown cosmetics just because the well-known, reputable brands are difficult to find. Instead, use your Oatine Beauty Creams with care, and you'll be surprised how long they last. What is more important, you'll retain your lovely complexion despite all wind and rain can do.

OATINE
BEAUTY CREAMS

Oatine Cream 2/8d and 5/3½d
Oatine Vanishing Snow 2/2½d
Oatine Powder Base 2/7d
including Purchase Tax.

OATINE, 357, KENNINGTON LANE, S.E.11

YOUR COUGH
HELPS THE ENEMY

A CHAIN is, proverbially, no stronger than its **weakest** link ; and it would be no great exaggeration to say that our war machine is only as strong as its weakest cog. The impaired fitness of a comparatively few of those engaged can seriously slow up the whole process of production. **Ill health postpones victory.**

Fortunately, science—which plays so large a part in modern warfare—has also proved swiftly progressive in the vital sphere of keeping the Nation fighting fit. Affections of the breathing organs provide notable examples of such medical progress. For instance, stubborn attacks of **Asthma** and **Bronchitis** can usually be checked almost immediately, nowadays.

In many cases, absenteeism resulting from such causes is easily avoidable ; the victim's sufferings are unnecessary—and therefore **un-patriotic** ; he is actually helping the enemy when a few pence would ensure unbroken service in the cause of Freedom.

For a 2d. stamp **the secret of the latest scientific methods of combating these distressing complaints is obtainable in simple booklet form from** Anestan Ltd. (Dept. A5), 59, Brook Street, London, W.I. **Never could two coppers be better spent in the joint interest of personal health and national security.**

Asthma
bouts checked ... ONE, TWO, THREE!
ANESTAN

stops that choking, straining, gasping for breath almost instantly *and* helps to mitigate future attacks. This is how it works :

1 It relaxes the rigid breathing muscle — usually within 30 seconds.

2 It loosens the hard, throttling phlegm, making room for grateful draughts of precious air.

3 It promotes sweet, undisturbed sleep, building up new strength and resistance.

Anestan's action is safe, sure and swift. Get it to-day and forget your Asthma fears. All registered chemists sell Anestan : 10 doses 2/-, 30 doses 4/6, 60 doses 7/10½, 180 doses 19/2—and these prices INCLUDE Purchase Tax.

Moreover, should you have any difficulty in obtaining Anestan, the proprietors will gladly arrange for immediate supplies to be sent to you post free.

ANESTAN, LTD.
(DEPT. A5),
59, BROOK ST., LONDON, W.1.

MINISTRY OF AGRICULTURE

A woman's place is in the – GARDEN

Women have done well in digging for victory. But the work must go on. There must be no letting up. More green vegetables must be grown for the children. They must have green vegetables to keep them bonny and free from disease — particularly in the winter. So grow plenty of cabbages, kale, sprouting broccoli, Brussels sprouts and leeks.

KNOW WHAT YOU ARE DOING

Don't just go about the job haphazardly. Send to the Ministry of Agriculture, Hotel Lindum, St. Anne's-on-Sea, Lancs, for these free leaflets.

HOW TO DIG. Dig for Victory Leaflet No. 20.

CROPPING PLAN. Dig for Victory Leaflet No. 1 for a 10-rod (300 sq. yd.) plot or No. 23 for a 5-rod plot.

HOW TO SOW SEEDS. Dig for Victory Leaflet No. 19.

If you haven't a garden, ask your local council if they can get you an allotment

The need is "GROWING"—

DIG FOR VICTORY STILL

POST THIS COUPON FOR FREE LEAFLETS

To Ministry of Agriculture (Dept. M.B.106), Hotel Lindum, St. Anne's-on-Sea, Lancs.

Please send me leaflets Nos.

NAME

ADDRESS

MY PEACE TERMS

A new type of government for Germany . . .

A fresh set of chair covers...

. . . and back to fresh butter, cream cheese and Crawford's Cream Crackers

Crawford's
BISCUITS
are **good** biscuits

WILLIAM CRAWFORD & SONS LTD., EDINBURGH, LIVERPOOL & LONDON

and has a similar readership profile. An English translation is given after the Swedish text.

The image used is of a well-known Swedish actress who has featured in serious dramatic roles.

As a reader situated within your own culture, how do you respond

Half-health's no good in the Navy! There's a job to be done and it needs fitness to do it.

— every morning take ENO'S "FRUIT SALT"

2/- and 3/6 a bottle (tax inc.)

THE MORE WE ARE TOGETHER

Wartime means living, eating, working and often sleeping in crowds — and this brings us all face to face with the problem of personal freshness. We simply dare not risk offending, but with heavy uniforms, close atmospheres, shortage of soap and of dress shields, the problem can only be met in one way — by the regular use of Liquid Odo-ro-no, the deodorant that gives complete protection from under-arm odour. In addition Odo-ro-no saves your clothes from perspiration stains and keeps uniform jackets, overalls and undies fresh and sweet. But remember, for absolute *certainty* of personal freshness it is essential you get Odo-ro-no — the original deodorant.

LIQUID

ODO-RO-NO

THE COMPLETE SHIELD AGAINST

UNDER-ARM ODOUR AND PERSPIRATION MARKS

You can obtain Odo-ro-no Liquid in two strengths. REGULAR (lasts for seven days), INSTANT (three days). In medium and small sizes.

to this advert: what is your reading of it? For example, do you see the image as a liberated expression of an individual woman's natural form, or is it exploitative of women as a group in depicting them in a particular way?

What kind of narratee is suggested by the verbal text?

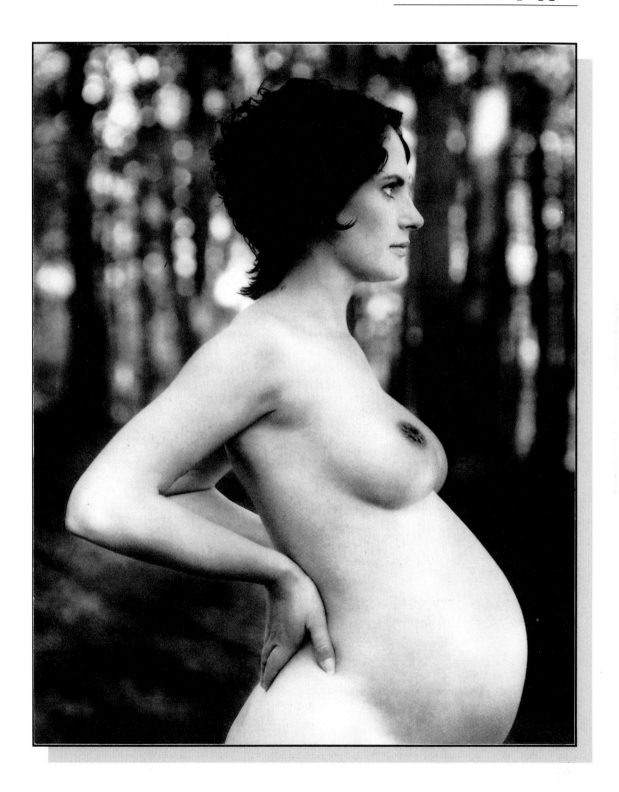

Text: Translation

RE/SOURCE. In every natural cycle it is necessary to make good use of existing limited resources. This applies to us human beings as well as to our natural resources.

The IL Waste Paper Recycling Company has a circulation system in which you are an important asset. Without you it cannot work.

Our recycling system is based on waste paper collected from companies and households throughout the country. New paper is produced from the waste paper, and the recycling process is kept going, a process in which you are the link between us and the waste paper.

For most people it comes as a matter of course to sort and return waste paper and this should be just as natural for companies, offices and shops. By recycling paper you can help us in many ways: to save energy and prevent the mountain of rubbish from growing even larger. Furthermore, the forests will last longer.

It is all so simple and so obvious. We will all gain from it, not least your children. Co-operate with IL Waste Paper Recycling Company and you will also be co-operating with the environment.

Would you like to know more? Call 020-257000 and we will send you a brochure.

IL Waste Paper for Recycling is the largest recycling company for paper in Scandinavia. The owners of IL Waste Paper for Recycling are five leading Swedish forest industry and paper manufacturers. Every year we deliver about 700,000 metric tons of waste paper to Swedish and foreign paper mills.

Commentary

The analysis below was written by Maria Forser, a Swedish university student following a course in English, during a module on language and culture. Her task was to choose an advertising text which she thought might raise interesting questions about culture, and to write about it for her audience, a student at a British University who was on a similar course.

Read the analysis and consider how similar or different the student's interpretation is to/from your own.

I chose this text because it has a lot of classical tricks at the same time as being an advert for a basically good thing.

The text is written in black on a white background except for 're' at the beginning, which is written in green, and the company name (Returpapper) at the end which is written in bright red. Green is the colour we associate with nature and all the environmental work we have today.

The text itself is a bit moralising, giving you the feeling that 'of course I know all about how to protect the environment and if I don't make all those arrangements about recycling and so on I ought to be ashamed of myself'. They use statements with an underlying message that 'but of course you already know all this, as the enlightened person you are'.

The advertiser wants to give you the impression that you cannot let them down as you are an important cog in a big wheel. The advertiser speaks directly to you, the caring and conscientious citizen who can, with help from this company, expand your work for the environment and introduce it to your office. The target audience for this advert are people who have an influence on the routines at their place of work.

The text appeals to our emotions and bad conscience about the way we treat our planet at the same time as being factual. They want the text to look serious. There are no obvious exaggerations and they mix flattering the audience by talking about their important role in the recycling process with the straight presentation of factual items. They have produced a black and white picture to endorse the idea of seriousness and to create an 'artistic' flavour at the same time.

Well, what about the picture? A beautiful pregnant woman symbolising life and the future? She is also standing in a forest. I don't think there is anything degrading and sexist about that idea. For me it shows a proud woman who is likely to be aware of the future because of the state she is in, but I know that many women would not approve of this picture: women are often shown as sex-objects or as reproduction containers. I think this is true, but I hope that some day a picture of a pregnant woman could be taken just for what it is. Also, one could argue that if they wanted to show a symbol of the future, they could have chosen something else – a child, for example. Therefore I believe that the fact that a naked woman is more likely to catch the reader's attention is the main factor in this case. I don't say that it is degrading but maybe the motive behind the choice of picture is a bit doubtful.

Is there something typically Swedish about this advert? That's difficult for me to say! Maybe we in Sweden like adverts that appeal to our 'better selves' with logical reasons – or, rather, we are fed with this from our authorities, so we have learned to expect and like it! It is almost like an advert from the National Board of Health and Welfare (except for the picture).

I guess this advert would be possible in all countries in western and northern Europe, but of course it would be out of the question in, for example, a Muslim country.

From time to time there are debates here about the way women are depicted in advertisements. Women are often objectified, it is said. If a man is present in the picture, he is often active and the woman is passive. He is taking care of things, she is taken care of. He has all the solutions and she is the one who applauds and is full of admiration. There have been successful campaigns against those kinds of adverts.

What was your *first* thought when you saw this advert? Is it OK to use naked bodies in advertising? (I'm not talking about those adverts that try to be sexy, or to use naked bodies in a degrading way.) And what do you think about the text – would it appeal to British readers?

If it is OK to use these kinds of pictures, where are all the naked men, I wonder?

Extension

This unit has examined ideas about cultural variation in terms both of different cultures and of different eras in the same culture. Below are some ideas for taking these aspects further.

1   If you have any access to advertisements in other cultures, compare an advert from that source with one for a similar product in Britain. You could also consider adverts that are in English, but from different cultures: for example, an American or Australian advert compared with a British one. Modern multinational companies often market exactly the same product in a number of different countries, and it is very revealing to look at the different strategies they use.

2   If you want to go further than a comparison on a product basis, you could explore the presentation of particular ideas across a range of advertisements in different cultures or through time within the

100

same culture. For example, answering Maria Forser's question about the use of naked bodies in adverts would entail a larger-scale investigation. This unit and Unit 5 each has a text featuring the idea of pregnancy: how does this idea appear in other contemporary British adverts, and how was this treated in older texts?

3   Compare the way a type of product advertises itself to different cultural groups within Britain: for example, hair-care products aimed at white women readers of, say, *Cosmopolitan*, compared with black women readers of *Ebony*.

4   If you want to explore ideas treated earlier in the unit, collect as many product brand names as you can find, and investigate patterns of sound and connotation: do certain types of product use particular groups of sounds? Do they use certain kinds of words, to try to evoke particular connotations?

Tricks of the trade

Aim of this unit

It should be clear from previous units that advertisements often rely on the fact that readers approach texts in an active way, being prepared to work to decode messages. This principle can operate at many different levels. For example, we saw in Unit 4 that some texts assume readers to be part of a spoken interaction where prosodic features have to be supplied in order for the text to make sense; Unit 5 considered the way readers understand texts in the light of other texts that are being referred to or implied. This unit continues to look at the same principle of the work that readers do, but the focus will be on a range of smaller-scale language features and strategies that recur within advertising texts.

TO COMPARE, OR NOT TO COMPARE

Advertisers tend not to make specific comparisons between their product and others by naming and referring to their rivals. So, for example, a washing powder manufacturer would be unlikely to say 'X washes whiter than Y'.

In linguistic terms, this construction is called **comparative reference**. It tells the reader that they need to locate particular items in the text, and draw them together for comparison on a specified basis. In the above example, this basis is 'whiteness'.

Their lack of specific reference to other products doesn't stop advertisers from employing comparative reference, however. What they do is to leave out the comparative item while keeping in the basis for comparison. So you get: 'X washes whiter'. We are not told 'than what', but as readers we tend to supply in brackets 'than all its other rivals'. To notice the way in which the reader works to provide a positive message as a kind of norm, try supplying some very unflattering comparisons: 'washes whiter than a sackful of coal', 'washes whiter than industrial effluent'. As readers, we are so used to making the missing element a positive one, that where advertisers could put the comparison in (such as where their product has been changed over time, so they are referring to themselves), they often don't have to bother: they just need to say their product is 'better' and we will provide the missing 'than ever before'. Perhaps advertisers are trying to have their cake and eat it here: there's always the chance that the reader may supply both possible comparative readings for 'better' – superior to all contemporary rivals, and much improved on previous versions of itself.

Advertisers don't always encode a 'more is better' idea, although for many products, particularly some ranges of food, this message is still the standard one. But it may also be the case that a product is claiming to reduce something – cost, daily wear and tear, hassle, embarrassment, and so on. Such claims also involve comparative reference, such as in the Mobil petrol 'diesel plus' slogan 'More poke, less smoke'. This suggests power without pollution, hence more of a desirable quality but less of an undesirable one. Supplying negative comparisons for this again shows up the work that readers do: for example, 'more poke than a bicycle, less smoke than a chemical factory'.

As well as constructing claims to comparative superiority, comparative reference can also feature in expressions of superlative excellence. The strategy works in the same way: 'simply the best' still requires us to supply the answer to 'best from which group of items?'

Activity

Below are some words that occur frequently as the basis for comparison in adverts.

Add to this list, then see if you can divide up the words according to the types of products they are normally attached to:

| newer | crunchier | better | crispier | healthier | nicer |

more satisfying   crumbliest   less fattening   smoother

the best   simpler   easier   more experienced   tastiest

BUZZ AND SPIN

Vocabulary items such as those you have been studying are important elements to consider in analysing adverts, for a number of reasons. They are often strongly connected with the product's proposed 'unique selling proposition' – the quality that makes the product a 'must' to buy. They also tend to be markers of what is thought important at the time. For example, in an age concerned with pollution, phrases such as 'a cleaner solution' and 'kinder to the environment' are likely to be received sympathetically, while our fears about the increasingly artificial nature of our food are met by expressions of 'naturalness' such as 'the purer choice', 'fewer additives' and 'a fresher taste'.

These terms have often been called 'buzz words', suggesting a kind of electrical charge as a result of making a connection, hitting the spot, having a finger on the pulse, pressing the right buttons. Terms change with time and with culture, as illustrated in Unit 6. The term 'buzz' itself now sounds out of date, with the contemporary word 'spin' more often used to mean 'constructing a favourable image' for something or someone, 'spin doctors' being the public relations gurus behind such fabrications.

The words in the list above are in their comparative form, but the adjectives at the base of the words ('new', 'easy', 'healthy') also occur frequently in adverts, of course. The difference is often where they occur: comparatives are more likely to feature in the advert slogan, while the adjectives in their base form often occur in the body of the text (called the 'copy'). Guy Cook (1992) makes a useful distinction between the kind of phrase that attaches to a product on all its adverts, whatever the campaign (for example, Carlsberg's 'Probably the best lager in the world'), which he calls a **slogo**, reserving the term **slogan** for phrases that come and go with particular lines of product and different campaigns. Here, 'slogo' uses the idea of the kind of permanent marker or identifying sign that distinguishes a whole company. This is the concept inherent in an advertising **logo**. For more on this, see Unit 8.

In analysing the descriptive terms used about a product, the principle of connotation needs particular investigation. For example,

105

while adjectives such as 'new', 'economical' and 'universal' may well be used, you would be unlikely to see the equivalents 'untried', 'cheap' and 'common'. Vocabulary is carefully chosen to promote positive associations in the minds of the target audience. Since audiences clearly differ in what profile they might want to have for themselves, the words chosen to describe the supposedly desired object or service will also vary. For example, the term 'expensive' is not one that you would think to see in an advertisement – who is likely to want to tell their audience that their product costs a lot of money? Yet a particular shirt manufacturer consistently tells the reader that its shirts are 'reassuringly expensive'. The connotations here are positive: the reader is encouraged to think that they are going to buy something that is beyond the reach of the *hoi polloi*. It is a privileged buy.

YOU'VE MADE IT TO THE TOP – BUT ARE YOUR ACHIEVEMENTS RECOGNISED?

The slogan (and slogo) used by a company selling a particular product will tie in closely with the descriptions used in the advertising copy. They will also relate to the hook – the initial piece of attention-seeking verbal language used to draw the reader in. Hooks often occur in question form, as above, which is the initial line of an advert selling membership of the Institute of Financial Accountants. The hook identifies a problem, which the copy then expands on:

> We recognise that many people with considerable financial skills have risen to the top echelons of their organisations, but do not have a professional qualification.

Having set out the problem, the advert suggests that the product can solve it. Most of the copy is taken up with describing the benefits of membership of the IFA.

A problem–solution format is characteristic of many advertisements, with the hook in the form of a question (or a statement) raising the 'problem' in the reader's mind. Problems can be wide-ranging, from body odour to lack of writing skills, and from childcare difficulties to workplace stress. Whatever the problem is, the friendly advertising copy suggests that the advertised product can sort it all out. The advertisement is our friend in times of trouble, in a difficult world where we don't get our just deserts.

106

In Text: Hooks (1) are some problem-raising hooks from contemporary adverts. How do these questions and statements play on the insecurities of the reader? Can you tell just from the hook whom the advert might be aimed at? Do you think different target audience groups – for example, men and women – are presented with different 'problems'?

Can you think of any more lines like these, either from written adverts or from TV commercials?

Text: Hooks (1)

Hook	Product
Thinning hair?	Hair restorer
Not enough hours in the day?	'Energy' drink
Hollywood's best kept secret: breast enhancement without surgery	Padded bra
Want to lose 4cm of bust projection instantly?	'Minimiser' bra
Nothing put by for a 'rainy day'?	Savings scheme
Could you work if you were disabled?	Insurance
Why are you shamed by your mistakes in English?	Language programme
Ever wanted a new 'you'?	Diet programme
Mum, why's Granny coming to live with us?	Pension scheme
Good looking. Reliable. Bright. (If only more men were like that).	Wristwatch
And what is it you're afraid of? That you might lose? What's to lose?	Trainers
Still shaving with soap and water?	Shaving gel
Age is a fact of life, but why look it?	Moisturiser
Why not get rid of the old boot for something more shapely?	Football boots
Your circumstances may have changed. Why should you?	Nursing home
He trusts his mum to get him home, but who can she trust? *(Image of a baby in a car seat)*	AA

COMING OFF THE PAGE

Targeting readers' insecurities with a carefully worded question at the start of an advertisement is another strategy for making the reader work. In the case of the hooks you have just been studying, the appeal is very much at the level of emotion, with readers fretting and worrying about themselves: Is my body the right shape? Do I have enough money put by? Who will look after me when I am old? What are my love relationships like? How can I protect my child?

Other hooks can be the prelude to a more cognitive appeal, where the brain is engaged in working out a puzzle. For example, here is the hook for a laptop computer: 'How is it possible to have a notebook without paper?' Selling a computer through a brain-teasing conundrum seems appropriate. However, there are current adverts for pieces of technology whose slogan is 'Technology, with love'. As soon as something becomes the norm in advertising, an advert can become new and startling by breaking out of the system it is in.

Written adverts have another way of teasing the brain, because of their very nature as written language. They can remain written language but, with the knowledge that we are using our 'inner voice' when we are reading, play themselves off against spoken language. This applies not just to hooks, but word play is likely to occur frequently in that position because of the hook's function as an attention-getter. Sometimes the play involves alterations of conventional spellings; sometimes changes in sounds are suggested (for example, **phoneme substitution**, where one sound is replaced by another); sometimes written elements regroup when spoken, producing new configurations and therefore new meanings.

Activity

In Text: Hooks (2) are some texts that contrast the way words sound with the way they are written, in order to engage the reader in a code-breaking exercise.

Explain how each of them works, including any intertextual references.

Text: Hooks (2)

Perrier: a bottle of water pictured at close of day
Hook: 5 o'clock shadeau

Braathens Airlines (a Norwegian company, advertising in Newcastle upon Tyne)
Hooks: Inspect a Norse
Fjord transit

Toothpaste
Hooks: Not just a pretty paste
Only ours lasts hours

Mouthwash
Hook: Plax worx

Ansells low alcohol drinks: image of a man dressed as a woman, standing under mistletoe
Hook: Ansells low alcohol drinks, so you won't get horribly kissed

Fila trainers
Hook: The best F in shoes

Fax machine (Image: page emerging from fax machine, with a romantic message on it)
Hook: Do you want a non-stop fax life?

Extension

This unit has explored various aspects of language that recur in written adverts, and any one of these aspects could provide the basis for collection and further research, involving TV adverts as well as written ones. The subjects covered were as follows:

1   The use of comparative reference
2   The connotations of words
3   Problem–solution discourses
4   The use of hook-lines
5   Playing off written language against its spoken equivalent.

109

In analysing your data, consider the ways in which linguistic strategies such as the above contribute to the larger picture constructed by the advertisement, particularly how the text constructs its narratees, and the role played by images in the overall message. In other words, don't let the items above be the end of the story.

Picture me this

Throughout this book, some consideration has been given to the importance of images and representation in the construction of advertising
messages. This unit will draw together some ideas, and focus in particular
on the way images form part of the way we 'read' a text.

In previous units, we have explored the way in which texts are often
interactive, in engaging the reader as one of the interlocutors in a
dialogue. We have seen, too, how readers are positioned as particular
types of people in becoming the narratees for the text. Images can play a
powerful role in suggesting how interactions occur and who the partici-
pants are.

Activity

Read Text: Allinson's. How does the image help to construct:

1   the way we read the interaction *in* the text?
2   the way we ourselves interact *with* the text?

Text: Allinson's

" I'm going to call this picture ' Portrait of a Gentleman with Sandwich.' "

" Make it ' Portrait of a Gentleman Enjoying Sandwich !' It's an outstanding sandwich. How did you learn it ? "

" Tradition of the family, my man. Handed down from mother to daughter."

" What's the secret ? "

" Oh, just talent I expect — and Allinson's bread."

" What's Allinson's got that the others haven't got ? "

" Lots. All the lovely vitamins and I don't know what else that are whipped out of ordinary flour before we ever get a chance at them."

" Well, even if it is good for me, I must say it's very pleasant to eat."

" The flour's amazingly fine, of course, something to do with being ground in the old-fashioned way by millstones."

" Splendid. Let's have another sandwich. It might give me strength to take the roller once over the lawn."

Commentary

The way we read the interaction *in* the text

We would understand that the text is presenting two speakers turn-taking even if the image were absent, because of the graphological signals of lighter and darker type, but the image helps us to construct a female referent for the first turn, and it sets the speech in the context of action: the first speaker is taking a photograph of her interlocutor, the 'gentleman' referred to in her first utterance. He is eating the sandwich she has made him; she is capturing him in mid-munch. We know she is photographing him rather than us, because of the angle of her vision. He appears to be sitting down, perhaps at a table, because her lens positions him in this way.

The verbal text plays with the idea of heritage and aristocracy: although he is referred to as a 'gentleman', it is she who has inherited riches – the sandwich-making expertise handed down from her mother, courtesy of Allinson's, of course. This is a 'modern' couple who can play with stuffy notions of social class and privilege by parodying classical art ('Portrait of a Gentleman' in this case will be a photo-snap rather than an oil painting) and the idea of family artefacts (sandwiches, rather than the family silver).

The verbal language presents certain ideas about the speakers. Although the female speaker has longer turns, often in response to the male speaker's request for information, she downplays her expertise, claiming not to know things or knowing them only vaguely, through phrases such as 'I expect', 'I don't know what else', and 'something to do with'. The speakers' roles are also very stereotyped: the woman is feeding her man; he likes the sandwich despite the fact that it's doing him good; at the end, he is fortified enough to do some gardening.

The way we ourselves interact *with* the text

As readers, we are watching the scene described above take place. Although we are not being directly photographed by the female speaker, we are near the man – we could be sitting alongside him. To this extent, we are more in his domain than that of the woman. For male readers, this may result in feeling as though they are being constructed as the male participant; for female readers, the text can have a more complex interpretation. The female reader can be the photographer and therefore constructed as someone proud of her ability to satisfy her man; at the same time, she can be sitting near the man being photographed and feel vicariously what it's like to be on the receiving end of her own sandwich-making gifts. Given the publication this advert appeared in (*Woman and Home*), it would presumably be female readers who would be the target audience. For these readers, the advert then has an interesting duality: a carefree-sounding, anti-establishment woman who still feeds her man properly. Allinson's for the modern female consumer.

The reader is left to wonder if the photographer ever got to eat one of her own sandwiches.

This advert has illustrated that images work alongside the verbal text to create a whole reading, and that we should pay close attention to who is in the picture (and who is out of it). Images, like verbal text, do not arrive on the page by accident. Copywriters give careful consideration to the type of people they want to represent - or, it would be more accurate to say, to re-present, as every image is a re-presentation of something; it is never a 'natural' phenomenon. As soon as people are pictured, they become representative of the social groups they are seen to represent - groups such as gender, sexuality, age, ethnicity, social class, occupation and region. But the people are also not simply static pictures. They are part of the way the text interacts with us, the readers.

SYMBOLS

Images do not have to feature people in order to say something *about* people, however. Text: Lea & Perrins uses the idea of working-class traditional values, not by a recognisably human representation, but rather by a **symbol** - the famous Blackpool tower. This tower also stands for Lancashire, and hence for the regional dish of hot-pot that can be enhanced by a dash of Lea & Perrins sauce.

The advert suggests that Lancashire people are discriminating when it comes to homely nourishing food, only praising hot-pot with dialect adjectives (seen as 'genuine' language) such as 'gradely' and 'champion' if the dish is up to scratch - containing Lea & Perrins, of course.

The speakers in this text are an interesting mixture. We have a narrator who addresses us with a challenge about our hot-pot (notice the hook in the form of a question), but this voice is punctuated by a Lancashire speaker saying 'gradely', as if by fortuitous accident, from the tower.

We are not addressed by any Lancashire speakers: rather our narrator refers to them as 'they' and invokes them as a way of substantiating the idea of traditional wholesome cooking. In fact, the text treats Lancashire itself as if it can speak: 'Would *Lancashire* say ...'. This manages to remove the idea of individuals and suggest an identity for a whole area, making the verbal text match the symbolism inherent in the image of the tower.

Text: Lea & Perrins

Symbolic representation, such as the image of the Blackpool tower, can be a powerful source of meaning in texts of all kinds. Symbols are much more about associations of ideas than about any literal or straightforward equation, and much more about group convention than about individual personalised meaning. Such ideas are illustrated by, for example, the way we use the symbol of the heart to represent love, or the symbol of the dove to represent peace. You might argue that love makes the heart beat faster, but beyond that, the connection is somewhat tenuous. Similarly, the dove may remind us of a biblical story, but what has that to do with contemporary experiences of peace?

Symbols are culturally agreed conventions, so it is perfectly possible that in another culture, hearts could represent death and doves could be seen as vermin. Symbols also change over the years, as new groups use symbols in new ways. For example, the Nazi swastika was copied from an Indian religious sign signifying peace.

For all the reasons above, symbols are very useful to advertisers. Rather than the possible variations in meaning being a problem, they produce a useful fluidity. Loose associations are much more effective than watertight definitions. At the same time, symbols can be relied on to have predictable associations for particular groups, giving readers a sense of belonging and recognition.

Although symbols often feature in the main part of advertising copy, they do particular work by means of logos - the designs that companies use as their identifying mark.

Activity

The logos in Text: Symbols were all created in the 1980s, for the Prudential Insurance Company, the Minerva Publishing Company, and Powergen Electricity.

What ideas are suggested by these symbols?

Commentary

These symbols are all based on figures from classical mythology. However, their meaning is less about who these figures were, and more about the fact that they are perceived as 'classical' in the sense of traditional, longstanding markers of civilised life. Knowledge of classical literature, art and mythology has always been the province of the privileged elite, so these symbolic figures suggest very different ideas from, for example,

Text: Symbols

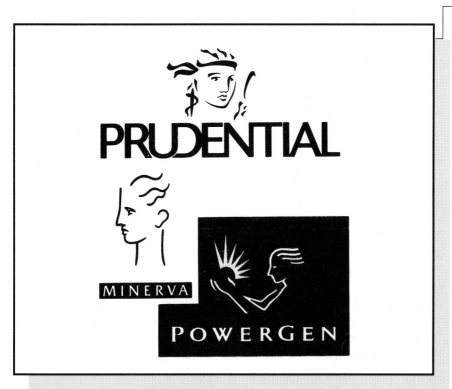

the Blackpool Tower in the Lea & Perrins advert. Although both the tower and these figures can symbolise tradition, they are very different traditions, with the Blackpool Tower standing for many years of working-class entertainment and leisure – the stuff of real people's lives. The classical figures are all god-like, ethereal figures, this idea being partly created by the nature of the line drawings. Ideas of grandness, ritual and power are suggested by the light controlled by the Powergen figure; the Prudential symbol is reminiscent of the Olympic games, with its Olympian torch and high ideals.

Even if we don't think any of the above when we look at these logos, we are still likely to consider these figures traditional because of their similarity to statues, and statues of classical figures still abound in our contemporary towns and cities. In fact, the Prudential figure was copied from a statue at the head office of the insurance company itself. Marina Warner (1985) makes the point that it is often female figures who stand in statuary for abstract qualities – like justice, equality and purity – while male figures are often just themselves, statues of real men who lived and

117

are being commemorated for some act in the real world. Interestingly, there is an association between the femaleness of the Prudential figure and the woman's name, Prudence, which itself encodes the abstract quality of careful foresight and, like Faith, Hope and Charity, was a popular Victorian name. In TV adverts the figure is sometimes called 'Prudence', and we are exhorted to 'ask Pru' (as opposed to asking 'the man from the Pru', which was the company's previous marketing strategy).

Another association some people might have for these figures is that of the art forms of the 1920s and 1930s, particularly in Fascist architecture. Hitler often called upon classical ideas and images to give himself higher status and to suggest that his empire was as grand as those of Ancient Greece and Rome. Whether companies such as the Prudential and Powergen would want to call up these associations is another matter. It is, however, tempting to look back on the plethora of figures such as these called into existence in the 1980s (think, for example, of the figure on BT phone boxes) and to see some connections between them and the right-wing politics of the time, all that was represented by the Thatcherite ideas of authority and leadership.

Symbols don't have to be removed from everyday experience to call up powerful ideas. We have many symbols around us that we interact with as part of negotiating our daily lives, and we probably don't see them as abstract at all: for example the symbol 'X', which can stand for 'wrong', a person's mark (as on a voting paper), 'multiply', and 'love', to name but four meanings. Again, such symbols have meaning because of a cultural agreement that this should be so. In this sense, symbols are no different from alphabetic letters. The area of **semiotics**, which is the study of signs in the widest sense (from road signs through verbal language to clothing and rituals in society), would refer to the symbol in question as the **signifier** and its meaning, including all the associations it calls up, as the **signified**.

Activity

Given all that has been said in this book about the way advertisements are constantly looking for new territory, it should come as no surprise that no symbol or sign is off limits for them – even our most humdrum road sign or mathematical symbol. This is the case in the series of adverts in Text: Bass, which featured as part of the Bass Ale campaign that ran during 1996.

Read the adverts and explain how the various signs and symbols are being used. As with all the other texts you have analysed in this book, consider issues of the relationships between narrators and narratees : for example, do any of the texts presume a male or female narratee? Also explore the kind of verbal language chosen, considering what effects are created by the choices made.

(Note : there is no commentary on this activity.)

Extension

The focus of this unit has been twofold :

1   The way images work alongside verbal text to construct certain ideas about the way the advert could be read
2   The nature of symbolic representation.

There is limitless potential in either of these areas for further data collection and research. For example, you could decide on a product type and investigate what sorts of images are used in the advertising of it. If you chose a product that is advertised to more than one target group, you could compare how the product is marketed to these different groups in terms of representation : for example, how do the images used in perfume (or 'fragrance') adverts aimed at men and women differ? Equally, you could pick a product type and collect as many logos as you can find, in order to discover whether the companies all suggest the same kinds of ideas. For example, do publishers use certain types of signifier? What is used by the publisher you are reading? Have a look!

Text: Bass

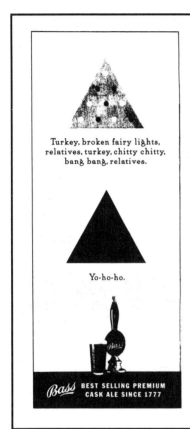

Turkey, broken fairy lights, relatives, turkey, chitty chitty, bang bang, relatives.

Yo-ho-ho.

Hump bridge.

Leave the bridge well alone.

Peace, love, flowers.

Beer.

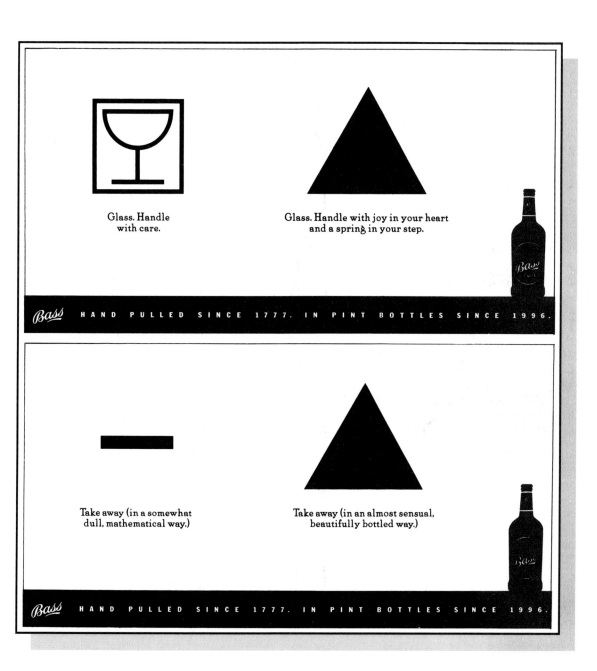

Glass. Handle
with care.

Glass. Handle with joy in your heart
and a spring in your step.

Bass HAND PULLED SINCE 1777. IN PINT BOTTLES SINCE 1996.

Take away (in a somewhat
dull, mathematical way.)

Take away (in an almost sensual,
beautifully bottled way.)

Bass HAND PULLED SINCE 1777. IN PINT BOTTLES SINCE 1996.

index of terms

This is a form of combined glossary and index. Listed below are some of the main key terms used in the book, together with brief definitions for purposes of reference. The page references will normally take you to the first use of the term in the book, where it will be usually shown in **bold**. In some cases, however, understanding of the term can be helped by exploring its uses in more than one place in the book, and accordingly more than one page reference is given.

comparative reference   104

While reference in a general sense means referring to something, comparative reference establishes a reference which is about making a comparison of some sort. For example, 'Her car is newer than yours' links the two cars on the comparative basis of 'newness'.

connotation   23

The connotations of a word are the association it creates. For example, the connotations of 'December', mainly within British and North American culture, would be of 'cold', 'dark nights' and 'Christmas Parties.' Because associations are powerful, fluid (and often covert) aspects of meaning, advertisers pay particular attention to this aspect of language.
See also Units 6 and 7.

copy adaptation   80

Text or, in advertising terms, 'copy', is said to be adapted, rather than translated, when it cannot simply be translated in a word-for-word way, but rather some consideration has to be given to the overall approach or message of the text, to see if that is likely to work with the target culture.

deictics   41

Words which point in various directions, both within a text and beyond it - for example, 'over here', 'down there', 'this', 'that', 'all you people out there' - and which serve to locate a speaker or writer in relation to what is said.

denotation   81

The literal, dictionary definition of a word, its barest factual meaning.

ellipsis   42

The omission of part of a structure. In face-to-face interactions, ellipsis is normally used for reasons of economy and can often create a sense of informality. For example, in the exchange:

'Ready?'
'Two minutes'

the ellipted elements are 'Are you' and 'I will be ready in' respectively, with the ellipsis here creating a casual and informal effect. Advertising language often attempts to reproduce the elliptical nature of spoken language in order to establish closeness with the reader.

euphemism   84

A polite which seeks to avoid directly naming an idea which makes speakers uncomfortable. Such ideas in Western culture are thought to revolve round bodily functions, sex, death and religion. These areas are also the source of our swear words, since they derive their effect from the breaking of taboo, or areas which are 'forbidden'.
The opposite of euphemism is dysphemism: for example, in words for sex, 'making love' and 'sleeping with' are euphemistic, 'shag' is dysphemistic.

123

features 46
The characteristics of language, how it appears, its shape and form.

first person (see **narrative point of view**)

functions 46
What language is used for, its purposes.

grammatically 43
Relating to the grammar of a language, or the rules and conventions for the way structures are combined. Norms of usage vary between spoken and written grammar: for example, speech tolerates – even expects – considerably more repetition than writing, where variation of structures tends to be more highly valued.

graphological 21
Relating to all the visual aspects of texts, including layout and images. See also Unit 8.

idiomatic language 83
Sequences of words which function as a single unit of meaning, and which can not normally be interpreted literally. For example, the sentence 'she is over the moon' contains the idiom 'over the moon' meaning 'happy'.

interaction markers 44
Features of speech that show evidence of the nature of spoken language as a two-way process, for example interruptions and overlaps.

intertextuality 69
The way in which one text echoes or refers to another text. For example, an advertisement which stated 'To be in Florida in winter, or not to be in Florida in winter' would contain an intertextual reference to a key speech in Shakespeare's *Hamlet*. Intertextuality can operate at many different levels of language, from phonological and lexical references in titles and slogans to visual aspects such as layouts and images.

lexis 42
The vocabulary system of a language.

The nature of lexis and lexical patterns tend to be different in spoken, compared with written, language.

logo 105
A design or mark used as a company's permanent trademark, for example BT's figure of the piper. See also Unit 8.

metaphorical 83
A metaphor is a word or phrase which establishes a comparison or analogy between one object or idea and another. For example, 'I *demolished* his argument' contains a comparison between argument and war, also underlining the idea that arguments can be constructed like buildings.

narrative point of view 28
The way in which the language of a text sets up a relationship between the person who appears to be addressing us (the **narrator**) and the person being addressed (the **narratee**). For example, the narrator may use **first person** pronouns 'I' or 'we', in which case the relationship may appear closer and more personal than if **third person** address is used (the pronouns 'he', 'she', 'it'), which can often sound more removed and distant.

narrator (see **narrative point of view**)

narratees (see **narrative point of view**)

non-fluency features 44
Features of spoken language which interrupt the flow: for example hesitations, false starts, switching structures half-way through an utterance. Such features should not be considered 'mistakes', because we expect them to be present in informal conversation, to the extent that if a speaker does not reproduce them we regard the speaker as rather too smooth and glib.

paralanguage 15
Aspects of communication that work alongside verbal language: for example body posture, eye contact, facial expression.

124

Some texts define this area as more narrowly linguistic, focusing more on tone of voice.

phoneme substitution (see **phonological**)

phonological   18, 108

Relating to phonology, the sound system of a language. A phoneme is a single unit of sound. **Phoneme substitution** is the replacement of an expected sound by an unexpected one, for deliberate effect. Advertising often uses this strategy, as do 'corny' jokes, for example:

Q. What newspaper do cats read?
A. The Mews of the World.

See also Unit 4.

polysemy   83

A semantic process by which certain words have several meanings. For example, the word 'chip' is polysemous.

presupposition   52

Ideas that are taken for granted in language, without which utterances would be very uneconomic. For example, the utterance 'Have you stopped dieting?' contains the presupposition 'You were dieting.' (Depending on the context, it could also mean 'You're looking a bit fat again!') Presupposition is all about reading between the lines; since this is, as it suggests, a hidden process, it is very interesting to advertisers, as we can be taking in all sorts of assumptions without consciously paying attention to them.

prosodic features   42

Features of spoken language, such as stress and tempo, that make up its overall rhythm and melody. Prosody is language-specific: you can get something of the feel of this when you listen to a foreign language you are unfamiliar with on a radio station.

pun   66, 83

A comic play on words as a result of a word having more than one meaning (see **polysemy**, above) or two words with

different meanings having the same sound. The latter is called *homophony*, and an example would be the two words 'great' and 'grate'. Shop titles often use homophony: for example, a fireplace shop could be called 'Grate Expectations'.

semiotics   118

Human communication through signs and symbols, from the small items such as those seen in company logos to larger signs such as clothing and social rituals. In semiotics, the term 'sign' is used with the widest meaning of 'something that has significance'; the sign itself is termed the **signifier** and what it communicates is termed the **signified**. For example, a black leather jacket of a certain type could be a signifier for the signified meaning of '(youthful) rebellion'. Some texts distinguish between different types of sign, those having a loose association with a referent being termed a 'symbol', while those that are more of a direct picture, such as a map or many types of roadsign, are termed an 'icon'.

signified, signifier (see **semiotics**)

slogan   105

A phrase designed to be memorable, attaching to a product or service during a particular advertising campaign; in this book (after Cook 1992), the term **slogo** is suggested for a phrase which is used by a company throughout all its advertising, regardless of the campaign. An example of a slogan is BT's current 'It's good to talk.'

slogo (see **slogan**)

sound symbolism   83

The process of association between a sound or sequence of sounds and an idea, for example the use of 's' sounds to suggest the sea. There is no natural connection between sound and meaning beyond that established by cultural convention.

Speech Act Theory   52

The idea that speech is action or

125

behaviour. For example, when someone says 'I swear to tell the truth', they are performing an action. This theoretical area also explores the assumptions we make when we have a conversation (see **presupposition**).

stereotyping 62

Attributing a range of fixed characteristics to individuals on the basis of their group membership.

taboo (see **euphemism**)

third person (see **narrative point of view**)

topic changes 44

Switches from one subject to another. Topic changes work very differently in speech and in writing, spoken language being much more able than written language to range across a number of topics in a short space of time. In speech, topic changes are often related to the operation of turn-taking, as new speakers will typically use their turn to take the conversation in a new direction. (See also **turn-taking**).

turn-taking 44

An aspect of spoken language whereby speakers co-operate with each other to maintain the participative nature of interactions.

typographical 17

Relating to aspects of typeface, for example different print sizes, fonts and styles.

Unique Selling Proposition 4

A characteristic of a product which is thought to separate it from its rivals.

further reading

There are some older texts on advertising that have stood the test of time. Among these are the following:

Goffman, E. (1979) *Gender Advertisements*. Harper & Row.

Williamson, J. (1978) *Decoding Advertisements : Ideology and Meaning in Advertising*. Marion Boyars.

A more contemporary book with a specifically language focus is the following:

Cook, G. (1992) *The Discourse of Advertising*. Routledge.
This book looks in more detail at many of the aspects dealt with here (including the relevance of Speech Act Theory), and also covers TV advertising.

If you are interested in the aspects of point of view covered in this book, then the following would be useful:

Simpson, P. (1993) *Language, Ideology and Point of View*. Routledge.

A book which looks at advertising discourse as part of the larger subject of language and power is:

Fairclough, N. (1989) *Language and Power*. Routledge.

Also considering advertising, but with a focus on gender, is the following:

Mills, S. (1995) *Feminist Stylistics*. Routledge.

The way in which advertising can be placed within a framework of written textual variation is covered in:

Bex, T. (1996) *Variety in Written English*. Routledge.

The role of context and audience in determining textual meanings is given more extensive treatment in:

Schirato, T. and Yell, S. (1997), *Cultural Literacies*, Allen & Unwin.

If you would like to investigate the area of images further, then have a look at:

Kress, G. and Van Leeuwen, T. (1996) *Reading Images : The Grammar of Visual Design*. Routledge.

A good starting point for understanding semiotics is:

Barthes, R. (1993) *Mythologies*. Vintage.

Books on general aspects of language are too numerous to list here, but if you want to support and check your understanding of some of the basic concepts and terms referred to in this book and in the core book which accompanies this series, then the following reference books are recommended:

Crystal, D. (1991) *A Dictionary of Linguistics and Phonetics*. Blackwell.

Crystal, D. (1995) *The Encyclopedia of the English Language*. Cambridge.

references

Brierley, S. (1995) *The Advertiser's Handbook*. Routledge.
Cook, G. (1992) *The Discourse of Advertising*. Routledge.
Crystal, D. and Davy, D. (1969) *Investigating English Style*. Longman.
Sebag-Montefiore, H. (1987) 'The Bottom Line', *Sunday Times*, 7 February.
Warner, M. (1985) *Monuments and Maidens : The Allegory of the Female Form*. Picador.